Disclaimer: The opinions presented herein are solely those of the author except where specifically noted. Nothing in the book should be construed as investment advice or guidance, as it is not intended as investment advice or guidance, nor is it offered as such. Nothing in the book should be construed as a recommendation to buy or sell any financial or physical asset. It is solely the opinion of the writer, who is not an investment professional. The strategies presented in the book may be unsuitable for you, and you should consult a professional where such consultation is appropriate. The publisher/author disclaims any implied warranty or applicability of the contents for any particular purpose. The publisher/author shall not be liable for any commercial or incidental damages of any kind or nature.

First edition published November 2012

Oftwominds.com
P.O. Box 4727
Berkeley, California 94704

Why Things Are Falling Apart and What We Can Do About It

Charles Hugh Smith

With gratitude to my lifelong friends Gary Baker and Jim Erler for their interest in oftwominds.com, and to correspondents Bart Dessart (Australia), Mark Gallmeier, Lew Glendenning, Zeus Yiamouyiannis (U.S.A.) and Simon Hodges (U.K.) for sharing their understanding of the concepts presented in sections 5 and 6, Understanding Systems and What We Can Do About It.

Table of Contents

Introduction

Things are falling apart—that is obvious to everyone but paid cheerleaders of the Status Quo.

Why are they falling apart? The conventional answer is a few "bad eggs" in our financial system triggered a recession that just won't end.

The correct answer is that the U.S. economy and society have structural problems that cannot be solved within the current Status Quo.

What can we do about it? We must embrace the fact that complex systems with diminishing returns will revert to simpler, lower costs systems either by collapsing under their own weight or by being replaced by systems that are faster, better and more sustainable.

Protecting vested interests at the expense of the average citizen is a key reason why things are falling apart. When people lose faith in the institutions that were supposed to protect them, when they feel that they have little recourse against abuses of power, the social fabric of the society falls apart.

Capitalism is based on a handful of principles: capital is invested—placed at risk—to earn a return. The marketplace is transparent to buyers, sellers and regulators. The market prices goods, services, risks and interest rates. "Creative destruction" eliminates inefficient, unproductive enterprises and frees the trapped capital to be deployed in more productive ways.

When vested interests keep failed systems from collapsing, creative destruction is not allowed to reallocate capital and labor.

When vested interests protect their monopoly from market forces, it acts like a hidden tax on our economy: the cost is spread to everyone. Protecting vested interests creates distortions that eventually bring the entire economy to its knees. When risk and consequence have been eliminated for the favored few, the system itself collapses.

But even if we eliminated the legalized looting of vested interests, our future is endangered by much deeper flaws in the Status Quo. We are becoming poorer, not just from financial over-reach, but from fundamental forces that are not easy to identify or understand.

The purpose of this book is to explain those fundamental forces so we can change what we leave future generations.

It is human nature to want to blame others. Yes, self-serving vested interests are eroding our society and economy. But it's not that simple: it is the entire Status Quo which is robbing future generations.

People tell me that the reason they like my weblog is that I make complex topics understandable. This is my trade, and I learned it over 25 years of free-lance journalism.

The only way to understand complex systems is to break them down into core concepts that act like "building blocks." Once we assemble these key concepts, we will have a solid understanding of our nation's problems.

I call this an *integrated understanding* because all the problems are related. It's the difference between understanding all the systems in a vehicle—the engine, fuel and electrical systems, brakes, transmission, heating and cooling, electronics, suspension and so on—and knowing that the car moves forward when you press the accelerator pedal. The person whose understanding is limited to pressing the accelerator pedal has no clue how to fix the car when it breaks down; they are helpless.

We will cover the five core reasons why things are falling apart:
1. Debt and financialization
2. Crony capitalism and the elimination of accountability
3. Diminishing returns
4. Centralization
5. Technological, financial and demographic changes in our economy

We will then cover what we can do to change an unsustainable future into a sustainable one.

One of the core ideas in this book (and in all my books) is that we are not powerless. Just because we are not individually rich and powerful does not mean we have no power. The Status Quo depends on us passively playing our role as consumers and taxpayers and allowing the vested interests to control the nation's finances and politics. Just as each vote we cast in an election is a vote for or against the Status Quo, every dollar we spend is a "vote," too. Every dollar we don't send to a vested interest is a dollar we can invest in our own household.

If we don't insist on change, then nothing will change, and things will fall apart. Not accepting responsibility and being powerless are two sides of the same coin: once we accept responsibility, we become powerful.

First we have to understand what's really going on, and then we have to accept responsibility to do two things: 1) change our daily lives to support what is sustainable, adaptable and open and 2) insist positive changes are made to the nation's bankrupt financial and political systems.

Section One:
Understanding Debt, Money and Leverage

We cannot possibly understand why things are falling apart unless we understand how debt, risk and leverage work, so we'll cover these fundamentals first. Entire shelves of books have been written on these topics, but since this book is designed to be read at the end of a long day, we'll cover these basics in a few pages. They really aren't that complicated once you boil them down.

But before we get to that, we need to cover two things: why we resist admitting that things are falling apart, and why identifying incentives and disincentives is the key to finding real solutions.

Our Resistance to Admitting Things Are Falling Apart

The foundations of American life are falling apart, though most Americans won't acknowledge it in public. There are many reasons for this, but two stand out: one is that we naturally shy away from problems we can't control and the other is that optimism is a core American value. "Stop focusing on the negative" is the standard response to any position perceived as pessimistic.

Ironically, problems that are swept under the rug don't go away; they get worse.

The analogy most people understand is alcoholism and addiction. Ignoring the alcoholic's destructive behavior does not help either the alcoholic or those he is hurting. Those who sweep reality under the rug for the sake of appearances or to avoid having to deal with the problem are called enablers, because their acceptance of the Status Quo enables the destructive behavior to continue.

A third reason is that we're afraid that if things fall apart we won't get what was promised to us by the Status Quo: Social Security, Medicare, pensions, and other benefits. Rather than face the reality that the economy cannot possibly fulfill all the promises made to 307 million Americans, we choose to ignore this reality and "hope it sorts itself out."

Denial only allows problems to fester and spin out of control.

There are five other reasons we resist admitting things are falling apart:

1. We're basing our assessment on false data. The government understands this, and that's why official statistics such as the unemployment rate are fudged to appear "not so bad." The idea that a college education guarantees a good job is another widely accepted falsity, though it is no longer true.

2. Conformity. Studies have found that the need to "fit in" leads people to accept blatant falsehoods if the majority of those around them have already chosen the falsehood. This is the lesson of "the Emperor has no clothes": cowed by conformity, all the adult townspeople agreed the Emperor's new costume was magnificent. It took a non-conformist child to blurt the truth: the Emperor's clothes were a fiction, and he was actually buck-naked.

3. Inertia. People are like vehicles: when their controls are shut off, they will coast for a long time. If we don't consciously change course, we keep drifting in the same direction. Institutions are even worse; the standard response when "more of the same" no longer works is to do even more of the same. In other words, "do more of what has failed spectacularly." In engineering terms, this is called "run to failure:" if nobody changes direction, the car will run right off the cliff.

4. Overconfidence, also called hubris. This is the root of the phrase "pride goeth before a fall." The individual who is supremely confident in the superiority of his judgment is an individual who will ignore evidence that he might be wrong. Reality trumps arrogance every time, and so the prideful eventually fall ingloriously flat on their faces.

5. Studies confirm what we know from common sense: humans don't like being insincere. We're uncomfortable being a hypocrite. So when faced with a falsehood that we don't want to admit, we believe in the falsehood rather than be hypocritical. This is why politicians will sincerely mouth falsehoods (such as "the economy is recovering"); rather than admit it's false, they become "true believers" in the lie.

Things are falling apart, and anyone who is honest will admit that we are leaving our nation's children an unsustainable mess. The nation is financially bankrupt, and our political system is morally bankrupt. It is easier to ignore the reality that the middle class, healthcare, government, justice, employment, education and even our national sense of integrity are falling apart than it is to face the troubling facts.

It's easy to confuse faith and political ideology. We resist changing our minds, but changing our minds does not require changing our faith; rather, our faith is the bedrock that gives us the resolve to confront the unwelcome facts and make positive changes in our lives before less positive changes are forced on us and our children.

The final reason we resist admitting that things are falling apart is the American ideal of "no limits." There should be no limits on what each person can accomplish, on our prosperity, or on what we spend to help every generation. But unlimited is obviously unrealistic. The only money that is available to spend or invest comes from surplus: we produce goods and services, and after we subtract the costs of production what's left is surplus. That's all we have to spend in the real world. Surplus is not limitless, and so difficult trade-offs have to be made.

This is a key "building block" concept we will discuss later. If we don't understand surplus, we understand nothing, and we won't be able to fix anything.

We avoid this reality by borrowing sums of money that are beyond imagination; we can't get our minds around $1 trillion, yet we borrow much more than this each and every year to maintain the Status Quo, including Social Security, Medicare, Medicaid, national defense, and so on.

We all know borrowing huge sums of money every year is unsustainable, and this is true of households and nations alike. We know this but most people choose denial or believing in falsehoods to avoid making any changes that would reduce their share of Federal spending.

If we refuse to hide from this truth, then we have to admit that the costs of our cowardice fall on future generations.

Incentives, Disincentives and Unintended Consequences

It may seem too obvious to be useful, but the key to an analysis that actually leads to solutions is to identify the incentives (what behaviors and choices are encouraged or rewarded) and disincentives (what behaviors and choices are discouraged or punished) in the system.

The way our behavior is guided by incentives and disincentives is a key conceptual building block we must understand inside and out.

People don't respond to "maybes," they respond to the incentives and disincentives in the here and now. People do try to follow their ideals, but we don't live in an ideal world. If deception and cheating are rewarded and transparency and honesty are punished, more people will start lying and cheating. If the rewards to be gained by deception become outsized, then the majority of people will fudge the facts to reap a windfall.

Psychologists have found that people who are lying and cheating (fudging their income, debts, test scores, accomplishments, taxes due, etc.) have convinced themselves that they're basically honest. This goes back to the human preference for sincerity over honesty: we prefer to believe falsehoods rather than admit we're being hypocritical.

Psychologists have also found that if people see others reaping a windfall from cheating, they are motivated to follow the lead of the cheaters even though they consider themselves honest.

A conventional analysis of our society and culture looks at financial data such as gross domestic product (GDP) or at the policies of the two political parties. This is what one of my readers termed "the argument industry," the army of pundits and academics who make a living arguing endlessly about issues that will never be resolved by staged "debates."

The only useful way to analyze a system is to identify what behaviors and choices are rewarded and which ones are discouraged.

If a policy was intended to encourage something positive but ends up being negative, we call these "unintended consequences."

In other cases, the regulations intended to inhibit negative behavior are not enforced, or they are only enforced occasionally to convince the citizenry that the laws "are working."

Destructive behavior doesn't have to be encouraged; it just has to be allowed. Human greed will provide plenty of motivation.

There are many examples, but let's take a few that are relevant to the hollowed-out, corrupt economy we're currently leaving our children.

If financial crimes such as fraud and embezzlement are rarely detected and prosecuted, those with the opportunity to embezzle millions of dollars will privately calculate what is called a risk-return analysis. If I can embezzle millions of dollars, and am unlikely to get caught, that encourages me to pursue potential embezzlements. If the punishment if caught is minimal, for example, a $10,000 fine, then even if I am caught stealing $10 million, I will get to keep $9.9 million (I will spend $90,000 on attorney's fees to argue that "it was an oversight," and $10,000 to pay the fine.)

That $9.9 million looks like "free money," and people will pursue "free money."

The number of people on permanent Social Security Disability has skyrocketed in recent years as jobs have become scarcer. People look at the rewards—"free money" every month for life—and so they pursue becoming qualified for disability. There are plenty of TV commercials touting companies that will help with the qualification process, and once you qualify, you never have to find a job again.

That's a very powerful incentive to fudge whatever needs to be fudged to qualify for lifetime "free money."

This was not the intention of the program, of course; it was designed for people who were severely injured at work back when most people worked in physical-labor jobs in factories or farms. But in many subtle ways, the program has become easy to "game;" the disability claim is never revisited, the disabled are not encouraged to work at some sort of job they could do (people in wheelchairs can still do computer work, for example), and the penalties for fudging are low and rarely enforced.

In a classroom example, if cheating is rewarded with high test scores, while cheaters who are caught get off lightly, then students will accept that cheating is "the New Normal;" if it is officially prohibited but unenforced, it is quickly recognized as the New Normal.

This is the way all corrupt societies work. Corruption is against the law, and there are severe penalties against it, but nobody is ever prosecuted because bribes take care of everything. The system is self-perpetuating, and that's why systems that become corrupt are so difficult to set right: corruption feeds more corruption.

Corrupt countries have thousands of laws on the books, but they are ignored if you pay the bribe. In America, we have developed two sets of laws: one for the Financial and Political Elites (the equivalent of the feudal Aristocracy) and one for "the rest of us" (the equivalent of powerless peasants and serfs).

Many incentives are legal and require no fudging, for example, the tax deduction for interest payments on home mortgages. But this incentive has fueled the expansion of debt that is now hollowing out the economy. People may be able to deduct the interest, but much of their income is going to pay interest.

The deduction for mortgage interest was intended to encourage home ownership, but it also encourages over-indebtedness and speculation in housing.

As we go through all the reasons why things are falling apart, we have to identify the incentives and disincentives that exist in each circumstance. We can do this by asking:

1. What are the rewards and costs of each choice?
2. Does the reward outweigh the cost?
3. Are the regulations actively enforced? If not, the prohibited behavior is actually allowed.
4. Is there any accountability for actions?
5. What are the consequences for the society and economy as people pursue the incentives?

Those who are benefitting from the current incentives will fight to keep them in place, even if they are destructive for the nation as a whole.

The only real solution to any problem is to change the incentives and disincentives so positive behaviors are encouraged and destructive behaviors are discouraged.

As the government intervenes in the economy, it puts more and more incentives and disincentives in place. These policies are either designed to protect politically powerful vested interests or they are stop-gap measures rushed into law to "fix" something. Such politically expedient policies inevitably trigger unintended consequences. Policies that were intended to "help" end up being terribly destructive.

The most important example is the Federal Reserve's policy of keeping interest rates near-zero, called ZIRP (zero-interest rate policy).

The policy is intended to lower the cost of borrowing so people will be encouraged to buy autos, homes, etc. and businesses will be encouraged to expand.

But the policy's unintended consequences have been a catastrophe for the nation. Zero interest means savers and pension funds earn virtually no interest. Indeed, if we factor in inflation, savers are actually losing money.

Interest income is critical to insurance companies and pensions. Since they can't make money with cash, these companies are driven to gamble in the stock and bond markets, where they risk losing much of their capital.

Since savings is capital, and capital that can be invested or loaned is the basis of capitalism, the Federal Reserve's policy is undermining capitalism and the economy in fundamental ways.

What was designed to "help" people borrow more is actually destroying the economy. This is just one example of an unintended consequence of policies that create huge incentives for debt and speculation and equally huge disincentives to savings and prudent investing. We will look at this in more detail later.

We Can't Argue Our Way Out of the Hole

Our basic problem is very simple: borrowing 35% to 40% of our government's budget is unsustainable, and what's unsustainable will break down and be replaced by some arrangement that is sustainable. Spending only what we generate in surplus is sustainable. Everything else is not sustainable.

Wishing that borrowing 40% of our budget is sustainable won't make it sustainable. Wishing that we could just print all the money we want to spend doesn't make that "something for nothing" magic work in the real world.

It's been said that humans are natural-born lawyers. We're always ready to justify our own actions and argue that the responsibility lies elsewhere. With no legal training, kids are expert lawyers at a very early age, making impassioned arguments why it's not their fault and why they deserve something they want.

We don't outgrow the desire to argue our way out of a hole. But the real world isn't forgiving like Mom or Dad; you can argue all you want, but you're still in the bottom of the hole even if you "win" the argument. Reality doesn't care about whose fault it is or what we deserve. The only way to get out of the hole is to climb out the hard way.

We could summarize the process of growing up as learning to accept responsibility head-on and putting aside our childish instinct to justify our own self-interest.

Looking for others to blame is a dead-end. As Jesus said, "He who is without sin among you, let him be the first to cast a stone." We are all responsible for the world we're leaving our children, and blaming others for doing exactly what we have done—pursue our own self-interests—doesn't get us out of the hole.

Sometimes what appears to be in our self-interest is actually self-destructive. We'll explore this later in "the tragedy of the commons."

The Chinese have an apt saying: If you're thirsty, it's too late to dig a well. If we keep thinking we can argue our way out of the financial hole, we won't have enough time or strength to climb out.

Why Do We Borrow Money?

Why do we borrow money? The answer may seem obvious, but we're like fish swimming in a sea of debt: the debt is like the water we no longer even see. Since we're trying to understand debt, we first need to understand why we borrow money.

We borrow money for three basic reasons:

1. We want to buy something that is so expensive that we can't save enough to buy it, such a house or a vehicle.

2. We want to buy something now rather than wait until we've saved money to buy it.

3. We're broke and are borrowing money to get by, and we have no way to pay back the money we're borrowing.

Credit and debt describe the same process: borrowing money. A bank offers you credit (as with a credit card) and you use the credit to buy something. You have taken on a debt. The bank is the creditor and you are the debtor.

In the old days, people saved 50% of the cost of a home as the down payment, and home mortgages (borrowed money) were only 50% of the cost of the house. Mortgages were designed to be paid off in ten years, not thirty years.

In previous generations, people used credit sparingly because credit was hard to get, and debt was understood to be a kind of slavery or servitude. People saved money in order to buy things, and the focus was on acquiring the necessities of life rather than instantly gratifying desires.

In many Asian countries, households routinely save 30% to 40% of their income. In America, households save 3% to 4% of their income, though a generation ago the savings rate was over 10%.

If you're only saving 3% of your income, it takes a long time to save enough money to buy something expensive. If you're saving 30%, then the money piles up 10 times faster, so the time needed to save a large amount is much shorter. Clearly, saving a large percentage of your income is the fastest way to buy something that costs a lot of money.

Why has America changed from a nation of savers to a nation of debtors? There are three reasons for this.

1. The government (what is called the Central State in political science) has guaranteed us all pensions and healthcare via Social Security and Medicare, so people no longer feel they have to save for their old age.

2. The income of 90% of American households has been flat for the past 40 years, once we adjust for inflation. Only the top 10%--the professional/managerial/investor class—has reaped real gains in income. The middle and working classes have compensated for stagnant income by borrowing money.

3. As described in the documentary *The Century of Self*, the development of psychology in the 20th century led to the perfection of propaganda and marketing. While propaganda was used to persuade entire nations to accept fascism and Communism, marketing and advertising in the U.S. transformed our culture from production to consumerism. Prosperity once meant having the needs of life fulfilled; now prosperity means expressing oneself through buying things. The

purpose of life is to fulfill wishes, not needs, and to "express our individuality" by buying things that define "who we are."

Needs are limited; after all, we can only eat so much food every day, no matter how much is available. Desires, on the other hand, are unlimited; there is no limit to the number of things or experiences we can desire.

While desires are unlimited, money is not unlimited, especially for the 90% of households whose income has been flat for the past 40 years. Costs have risen much faster than income, especially for higher education, healthcare and energy.

The "solution" to the "problem" posed by marketing—our desires are now unlimited, but our income remains limited—is to borrow money, and keep borrowing money until we can't borrow any more. We have followed this path not just as individuals and households, but as a nation. As our debts threaten to crush us, many people claim that the "solution" to our over-indebtedness is to borrow more money. In the following pages we learn why this can't work, and why it leads to national bankruptcy.

We have reached the third reason to borrow: we're broke, and so we're borrowing money that we know we will never be able to pay back. Is this really the world we want to leave our children?

Debt and "Least Effort for the Largest Gain"

All organisms share certain characteristics, and one of them is laziness: there isn't enough "free food" floating around for most organisms to waste energy on inessential activity. Since the word "laziness" has negative connotations, let's say Nature favors "the least effort for the largest gain."

Stream trout are a good example: the trout feed off the "conveyor belt" of food delivered by the current, but the trout don't waste energy fighting the fast-moving water: they hover nearby, behind rocks and in eddies, staying close enough to feed but in a manner that conserves energy, i.e. the least effort for the largest gain.

Human nature is famously two-sided: we have the inherent capacity for both good and evil, and many other opposing characteristics: we are competitive and cooperative, dominating and subservient, aggressive and passive, and active and lazy.

Like trout and all other organisms, we prefer "least effort for the largest gain" over risky, taxing endeavors, and there is no greater gain for the least effort than getting free money. If the government offers free money (for healthcare, food stamps, welfare, disability claims, corporate welfare, bailouts, subsidies, tax loopholes, etc.), we cheerfully grab it all.

In Nature, "free" is usually a one-time event, what we call a windfall. A crow happens upon a dead carcass, a tiger spots a crippled prey or a human stumbles on a tree loaded with fruit or a lake crowded with fish. After we feast on the windfall, we move on.

Government "free money" is not a one-time event; it is a permanent flow of free cash. When the free money never stops coming, it breeds an entitlement mentality, and the recipient loses the ability to fend for themselves in the real world. We see this in zoo animals; once they no longer have to "work" for their meals, they lose essential survival skills.

Humans who become dependent on free money enter a debilitating state where the way to "get more" is to make excuses rather than take risks in the real world. This takes much less energy than earning a living, and so our preference for "least effort for the largest gain" feeds an adolescent-like dependence and entitlement.

This is the dark side of dependency, and we see it in individuals, households and enterprises. When a wealthy young person collects a "trust fund" payment every month, they often become dabblers and dilettantes who pursue an interest for a time and then switch to another distraction. They never finish anything or accomplish much because ultimately, they don't have to.

When individuals get free money, their efforts to earn a living soon become half-hearted "going through the motions."

Companies that are dependent on government contracts soon lose the ability to compete in the real world, and banks that depend on government bailouts and Federal Reserve "free money" lose the ability to manage risk. As a result, they make bets and loans that inevitably lead to losses that fall on the taxpayers.

The great irony in human nature is that though we favor the "least effort for the largest gain," we only thrive when we're pursuing meaningful goals within a group that recognizes our contribution.

We will discuss this later, but for now the point is that debt appeals to our lazy-windfall nature: why sacrifice to save and work hard for more income when you can just borrow the money and get what you want right now with a "low monthly payment"? Why make difficult trade-offs when we can "have it all" by borrowing money?

On a national level, this has led to us to support politicians who promise us entitlements paid with borrowed money. We vote against politicians who report that we can't keep spending money that is borrowed from our children and grandchildren.

The surest way to lose popularity in a roomful of spoiled teens is to declare the era of free lunch money is over. In a democracy of debt-addicts, the truth-teller loses to the slick marketer who promises the free lunch will never run out because we can always borrow more money. "Popularity contest" elections where the candidates tell audiences what they want to hear do not enforce reality; rather, they enable debt-addicts to run the country into the ground.

This is the cost of becoming dependent on debt: eventually the borrower becomes an addict, blind to reality, living in a fantasy world and focused on one thing: getting more of the drug, which in this case is borrowed money. Only bankruptcy returns the borrower to reality.

The key adult skills in life are taking responsibility, being accountable and making difficult trade-offs.
Free money and easy credit erode these skills and feed a destructive dependency on debt.

Ever-Increasing Debt: To Whose Benefit?

A key question to ask of any policy is the Latin phrase, "Cui bono?" which means, "to whose benefit?" Every policy is sold as being "good for the country," but underneath the happy-story public relations, some vested interest is benefiting directly. We don't know who cooked up the policy, but we know a vested interest bought political power to make it law.

Who benefits from the Federal Reserve's policy of keeping interest rates near-zero for savers and banks? Not savers or pension funds; they are being driven into risky assets such as stocks in a desperation bid to earn a yield above 0%. If the stock market goes down, they will lose a lot of their precious capital.

Who benefits from Federal Reserve policies? The banks, of course, for they borrow money from the Federal Reserve for 0% and then loan it to us at 8% for student loans or 18% for credit cards.

Who benefits when the nation becomes dependent on borrowing more money every year just to get by? The banks, of course, who make money issuing new debt (loans and bonds). Few people understand that the banks make money when the U.S. Treasury sells new bonds, as the Treasury depends on a select few broker-dealer banks to sell the bonds in the international market.

Who ends up owning all this debt and collecting the tens of billions of dollars of interest? The "too big to fail" banks own most of the nation's home mortgages and credit card debt, and wealthy financial Elites own most of the student loans and much of the U.S. Treasury debt.

How much of the country do banks own? Bank assets exceed the entire U.S. gross domestic product ($15 trillion).

A nation that is dependent on borrowing more money each and every year just to get by ends up being owned by the banks, because the banks make money issuing the debt, servicing the debt and owning the debt. As more and more of the nation's income is devoted to paying interest, that income flows right to the banks and financial Elites.

This is why debt is so dangerous to democracy: once the financial Elites own most of the assets and collects much of the income as interest, they can buy political power.

Our dependence on debt has turned America into a neofeudal society, where the financial Elites are the equivalent of Feudal Lords living in well-protected castles, while the debt-serfs (the rest of us) toil our entire lives paying interest on our own debt and paying taxes that are used to pay interest on the government's debts.

Borrowing trillions of dollars indentures our children to pay the interest for their entire lives.

The Status Quo tells us that "debt is not a problem" because the nation's economy will expand so much that the $52 trillion we owe in public and private debt will become relatively small. But after borrowing and spending $6 trillion, a sum twice the size of the entire German economy, in just four short years (2009-2012), the Federal government has nothing to show for that money: adjusted for inflation, the economy has flatlined.

In other words, the Status Quo promise that borrowing and spending trillions of dollars will expand the economy is an illusion, a fantasy. All we're doing is indenturing our children to those who own all this debt. This debt will never be paid back; it's now too large for that. All we can do is re-finance the debt at higher and higher interest rates, paying ever-increasing sums of money to the banks. This is debt-serfdom.

Borrowing more every year just to keep your head above water is a trap with no escape, because you have to keep paying the interest to keep your credit rating high enough to borrow more next year. Rising debt is a death-spiral, as your income is stagnant but more and more of your income goes to paying interest, leaving you less for investment and consumption. Eventually you cannot afford the interest payments and you default. But by then, you're impoverished.

That's the world we're leaving our children and grandchildren.

If there was no debt, the banks would lose their income and their power.

There is one solution: stop borrowing. Stop adding to the bank's power and income.

Our System: Bank Credit Enforced by the Central State

If we don't understand the fundamental basis of our economy, we will remain clueless as things fall apart. The American economy is based on *bank credit enforced by the Central State*. What does this mean? It means banks create credit which everyone is pushed to borrow so the banks will earn interest and transactions fees on the loans. The Central State (the Federal government and Federal Reserve) protects the banks' wealth and power by rewarding debt and bailing out the banks when their speculative bets render them insolvent.

Does the Federal Reserve loan money directly to households at 0%? No. Does the Federal Reserve issue student loans at 0%? No. The Fed gives the banks money at 0% which the banks then lend to households and students. The banks pocket the transaction fees and the billions of dollars in interest that the borrowers pay.

How does the government reward debt? It allows debtors to deduct their interest payments (mortgage interest) on their tax returns. Savers get taxed, debtors get lower taxes. Debt is encouraged; thrift and paying cash are discouraged. Why? Because paying cash deprives the banks of their immense profits from issuing loans.

If you think "enforce" is too strong a word, then consider student loans. The Fed gives banks free money at 0%, and bails them out with $16 trillion in free money when they go bust. The banks then loan students money at 7% or even 8.9%.

Can the student discharge these loans in bankruptcy, like other debt? No. the government enforces this debt for the entire life of the student; the student cannot discharge the debt, ever. They are debt-serfs, the modern equivalent of medieval serfs indentured to the nobility. In our system of bank credit enforced by the State, the banks are the new feudal Lords and the Federal government is the protector of the financial nobility.

When the nobility gets in financial trouble, the government gives them unlimited sums of money at 0%--totally free money. When the student debt-serfs get in trouble financially, they are hounded and harassed for the rest of their lives.

If this isn't enforcement of the bank credit system, then what is it?

The banking system and the government are in a partnership. The State benefits from debt because it too is a debtor, and the political Elites benefit from the millions of dollars lavished on them by the banks.

The Fed gives the banks trillions of dollars in free money, and the banks give millions of dollars in free money to politicians. This is the inevitable consequence of a system of bank credit enforced by the State.

Understanding Surplus

It's absolutely essential that we understand this simple fact: we can only spend surplus. Once we've spent the surplus, we can borrow money, but the interest payments come out of the surplus. The more we borrow, the more interest we pay, and the less surplus we have left to spend.

Let's take a small-scale family farm as an example. Those with a vegetable garden, think of your own garden on a larger scale.

It takes labor (work) and investment (seeds, fertilizer, equipment, fuel, water) to grow crops. Labor has a market value, and so does the crop: they can be traded or sold for cash. The value of the labor and the investment is our cost of production. Let's say our total production costs to plant, raise and harvest our crop are $10,000. When we harvest and sell our crop for $20,000, we have a surplus of $10,000. But we can't spend that entire surplus; we need to set aside seed and cash for the next production cycle. We need to save some surplus to invest in future production.

If we need $3,000 to invest in future production, we have a $7,000 surplus to spend or "consume," as in "consumers spend money."

That's all the money we have to spend. If we spend the $10,000, then we will go broke next year because we didn't set any cash aside to invest in future production. The saying is that we "ate the seed corn," that is, we consumed the money we needed for future production.

This is true of any enterprise. If a factory saves nothing for investment, when its tools wear out then its production will decline and the factory will close because there's no money to buy new tools. If a software company never invests in future products, its current products will become obsolete and the company will lose sales. When losses mount, the company has no choice but to shut down.

There are only three ways to increase the surplus available to consume (spend):

1. Cut production costs
2. Increase production
3. Sell each product for more money, i.e. increase the profit margin

In general, the only way to increase production is set aside even more surplus to invest in the future. In other words, reaping more surpluses in the future requires sacrifice: we have to spend less now to invest more in the future.

There is no way to "fool Mother Nature": we can only spend what we generate in surplus.

There is one way to "fool Mother Nature" and spend more than we have in surplus: borrow money. We can borrow and spend $5,000, and pay the interest on the loan out of the $7,000 surplus.

But you can't really "fool Mother Nature" for long, because borrowed money has to paid back with interest. Interest is insidious because it eats up our future seed corn without us even being aware of it until it's too late.

We Can Only Spend Surplus in Four Ways

There are only four ways we can spend our surplus:
1. Consume it
2. Waste it on friction and unproductive investments
3. Invest it in future production
4. Pay the interest and principal on loans

If we spend the entire surplus on consumption, friction and interest payments, there is none left to invest in the future, and the enterprise—household, business or nation—goes into a downward spiral of less surplus that leads to less productive investment which leads to less surplus and so on. This is called a self-reinforcing spiral, i.e. a "death spiral," or a positive feedback loop.

Friction

Friction is an insightful way to understand waste and inefficiency, and why things are falling apart.

Take a bicycle as an example. If you flatten the bike's tires, increasing the resistance between the rubber and the road, that increase in friction causes the bike to be a lot harder to push forward than a bicycle with inflated tires.

A bicycle with wheels that barely turn will be tossed aside when the rider realizes he can go faster by walking, and with much less effort, too.

Economies have friction, too, and when the friction increases to the point that much of the economy's surplus are being consumed in overcoming friction, then the system eventually freezes up and is abandoned, just like the friction-crippled bicycle.

What do we gain from friction? Nothing. It is pure waste.

How much of the U.S. economy is friction? We've grown so accustomed to our way of doing things that we tend to assume that the present system is the most efficient one possible. Much of that faith is based on the belief that we live in a market economy, where efficiency—what we might call faster, better, cheaper-- is rewarded.

But the reality is that much of our economy is rigged to benefit incredibly inefficient vested interests, which act like friction. This enormous friction is grinding down the U.S. economy. What we're told is an open market is in fact a rigged market.

The Cost of Friction: Ten Doctors, Twelve Billing Clerks

Since 20% of the U.S. economy is devoted to healthcare (what I term sickcare, since it profits from sickness, not health), let's start with an example of massive friction in the U.S. sickcare system. I recently received an email (one of many I get from doctors and nurses) from a physician who wrote that his group has ten doctors and twelve billing clerks who do nothing but fill out forms and try to collect payments from insurers and agencies.

Note that this does not include caregiving support staff such as nurses or assistants, or general-overhead staffing such as bookkeeping, tax preparation, reception, scheduling, janitorial, legal services, etc. It also doesn't include the cost of malpractice insurance coverage or the hidden costs of "defensive medicine," that is, the practice of medicine aimed at minimizing lawsuits or thwarting future claims of malpractice.

Common sense requires us to ask how big the billing department would be in a single-payer or a cash-only system. Common sense also requires us to ask whether this enormous cost of billing—claims, counter-claims, adjustments, revisions, negotiations, disputed settlements, regulatory filings, lawsuits, fraudulent claims, to name but a few facets of this friction—adds anything to the quality of patient care.

We all know the answer is zero: it adds nothing but expense. The reality is that roughly half of all our $2.5 trillion in healthcare expenses is either useless paper-shuffling, needless tests and procedures or outright fraud. If we also subtract malpractice and defensive-medicine costs, we can guesstimate that another 15% of the nation's ballooning healthcare costs are friction. This means two-thirds of the nation's healthcare costs are friction.

We have a real-world test of this: we can compare what we spend per person and what other advanced democracies spend per person. We find that Japan spends 36% of what America spends per person on healthcare. France, Germany, England and Australia spend roughly half of what we spend per person.

We know two-thirds of our spending is friction because Japan provides healthcare for its long-lived population for 36% of our cost per person. Clearly, it is possible to provide care for a third of what we spend.

To keep this bike moving requires a huge amount of money and energy. Since we don't have that much surplus, we're borrowing trillions of dollars to overcome the immense friction of waste and inefficiency.

The sources of friction can be found not just in what's visible, but in what lies beyond our line of sight, purposefully hidden by limited choices. This is the essence of the crony-capitalist U.S. economy: the choices of efficiency are not just unavailable; they are ruthlessly eliminated by the vested interests that profit from friction.

For a real-life example of limited choice, we might ask: is a choice between a greasy taco and a greasy burger really a choice?

Many Americans are beginning to realize this same non-choice defines the two political parties: both are for sale, and both defend a corrupt Status Quo at every turn. The only difference between the two is the nature of the "sweeteners" paid to their constituencies.

The elimination of competition by rigging markets is "the way things work" in America (and in all corrupt economies), but the question now is whether a system that is mostly friction is sustainable.

Right now, the U.S. is maintaining its flat-tire -economy by borrowing 10% of its gross domestic product (GDP) every year. The interest payments will have to be paid by future taxpayers, so in effect we are borrowing from our children and grandchildren.

Interest itself is a kind of friction; once the money is consumed, there's nothing left but the interest due. That is friction. By making our entire economy dependent on more and more debt, we have created a source of friction that will eventually freeze the machine.

Any system loaded with unproductive friction is running not just on borrowed money but on borrowed time.

The point here is that systems burdened with friction are vulnerable to any drop in the energy needed to keep them going. If you're riding a bicycle with flat tires and half-locked brakes, any decline in your effort will bring you to a dead halt. If you were riding a well-oiled, open-market machine with almost no friction, you could reduce your effort and still keep up a brisk speed.

Borrowing 100% of our entire economy every ten years just to pay the high cost of friction is not sustainable.

Understanding Malinvestment (Unproductive Investments)

Not all investments are equal. Some are very productive; others are "dead money" (also called stranded capital or trapped capital) that produce no return at all. These are called malinvestments.

Everybody knows that once borrowed money is spent on consumption, friction or lost bets, it's gone, and all that's left is the loan payment. That's why politicians always describe spending as "investments" because this sounds sensible and prudent. But much of what is passed off as "investment" in the U.S. is just friction or consumption. It actually isn't an investment at all.

A few examples will illuminate the difference between a productive investment and a "dead money" malinvestment.

A bridge that connects two halves of a city is an investment, as it makes commerce faster and cheaper. A "bridge to nowhere" in a remote location is a malinvestment.

We all understand a house is shelter. That is its intrinsic value. We also understand that comforts added to the house are not essential, and so they are forms of consumption. If I install fancy curtains in my house, this doesn't add to the value as shelter; it's a discretionary purchase.

But a house only has value as shelter if somebody wants to live in it and if they can afford to live in it. Let's say one person invests $500,000 in a large five-bedroom "McMansion" out in the middle of nowhere, far from jobs, hospitals, airports, public transit and schools. It has gold-plated faucets and a fancy kitchen, but it's so far from what people need that nobody wants to live there. Even worse, the cost to build it was so high that the owner has to charge a lot of rent, so few can afford to live there.

Another person invests the same money ($500,000) in a four-apartment building right in town. Since the apartments are close to things people need, there are plenty of people who want to live there. Since the apartments are modest in size and features, the rents are equally modest. Many families can afford the rent. The rents not only cover the mortgage and maintenance costs, they yield a return of 5% annually.

This is a productive investment: it provides desirable shelter at an affordable cost and generates a return for its investors.

The McMansion is ultimately a form of consumption, not an investment. The investor can't rent it for enough to pay the mortgage, so he defaults and the house is returned to the bank (lender). The bank can hold the house and let it fall into disrepair or it can try to sell it.

The house only has value as shelter. Since it is in an undesirable location, its fancy features and extra space have little value. If it is so large that it will cost a lot to heat and maintain, it will be less desirable than a more modest house. Due to the high cost of maintenance, its market value may be near-zero: there may be no buyers at any price.

If it sits vacant for very long, the cost of repairing it will be more than its value.

This is a classic malinvestment. Not only does it not generate a return on investment, it is ultimately an almost total loss. The $500,000 invested in constructing it was "dead money."

When people can borrow $500,000 with no money down at 2% interest, they are willing to "gamble" that a McMansion in the middle of nowhere can be built and sold for a profit. Their risk and cash invested are low. In effect, the risk has been transferred to the lender.

It's like gambling $500,000 in a casino but only being liable for $1,000 of the loss.

Let's say the government wants to create jobs, so it finances the construction of a large steel mill in town. But there are already two steel mills in the area, and other local governments are already building three more mills nearby. Even worse, the two mills are only running at half-capacity because demand has flattened.

This is called overcapacity. The last few steels mills built may never produce a single ingot of steel, because there isn't enough demand to even keep the existing mills busy. This is what is happening in China, and it's a classic example of malinvestment.

Since the government can transfer the risk of its investment "bets" to the taxpayers, the leaders have no risk and no capital of their own in the projects they gamble public money on. When the projects fail, the cost is paid by the taxpayers, not the government leadership. As a result, it's easy for them to gamble public money on risky investments.

It's like gambling in a casino and having someone else cover your losing bets. That makes it very easy to bet, and bet big. That's why malinvestment flourishes in "easy credit" eras where investors and governments can borrow a lot of money at very low rates of interest.

Malinvestment occurs when risks have been off-loaded onto others while all gains are yours to keep. In this happy circumstance, there is no rational reason to wager conservatively; betting on long shots with huge potential payouts makes sense, as does betting spectacular sums.

Low interest rates and easy credit incentivize (reward) high-risk gambles and malinvestments. Higher interest rates and prudent credit reward productive investments and make high-risk gambles much harder to make.

Malinvestment and Government Borrowing

Whenever the American economy slumps, the Federal government rushes to compensate for reduced private-sector demand (a word economists use for consumption) by borrowing and spending large sums of money. Basically, the government throws trillions of dollars around and hopes some of it will magically "grow the economy."

The Keynesian economists behind this massive borrowing and spending use academic words and impressive equations, and it might seem their policy is very sophisticated and complex. It's not. Their economic "religion" boils down to a very simple idea: they see borrowed money as fertilizer. Dump it pretty much anywhere and new seedlings of economic growth will magically arise.

Their phrase for magic fertilizer is "aggregate demand."

But as we've seen, money spent on friction is wasted; it doesn't grow anything but unproductive fraud and speculation. We've also seen that money dumped into malinvestments doesn't grow anything, either; a bridge to nowhere adds very little value to the economy, but the debt taken on to build it requires that we pay interest on the loan forever.

The Keynesians are a "cargo cult." After the U.S. won World War II in the Pacific Theater, its forces left huge stockpiles of goods behind on remote South Pacific islands because it wasn't worth taking it all back to America. After the Americans left, some islanders, nostalgic for the seemingly endless fleet of ships loaded with technological goodies, started Cargo Cults that believed bizarre rituals and incantations would bring the ships of "free" wealth back. Some mimicked technology by painting radio dials on rocks and using the phantom radio to "call back" the "free wealth" ships.

The Keynesians are like deluded members of a Cargo Cult. They ignore the reality of debt, rising interest payments and the resulting debt-serfdom in their belief that money spent indiscriminately on friction, fraud, speculation and malinvestment will magically call back the fleet of rapid growth.

Unfortunately, it's our children and grandchildren who will pay the price for the Keynesians' deluded belief in Cargo Cult magic.

To the Keynesian, a Bridge to Nowhere is equally worthy of borrowed money as a high-tech factory. They are unable to distinguish between sterile sand and fertilizer, and unable to grasp the fact that ever-rising debt leaves America a nation of wealthy banks and increasingly impoverished debt-serfs.

They do not understand diminishing returns, a key concept we will cover shortly.

Politicians label all government spending "investments," but very little actually qualify as investments in a business sense of generating a return on investment. Most government spending lines the pockets of vested interests, leaving little to show for the trillions borrowed and spent on friction and "dead money" malinvestments.

You cannot "borrow your way to wealth" if the money is wasted on friction, fraud and malinvestment.

The Casino: How Rising Risk Brings Down the Entire System

The economy's financial instability can be traced back to one simple rule of Nature: risk cannot be eliminated; it can only be transferred to others or hidden.

Once risk has been disconnected from consequence, then it is impossible to discover the price of risk. Once risk has been shifted to others, then the inevitable result is malinvestment (also called "misallocation of capital").

In what we might call real capitalism, as opposed to crony-capitalism, risk has consequences. If the risky investment pays off, the consequence is profit. If the investment sours, the consequence is loss.

The only way to know how much cash should be put down on a loan and what interest rate to charge is to price the risk by placing the borrower's offer on an open market where lenders can bid for the loan. Those who see it as a risky investment will demand a large down payment and high interest, while those who see it as a safe investment will ask for a smaller down payment and lower interest.

This process is called "price discovery," and it's what open markets do. The risk of the intended investment is "discovered" by truthfully describing the project and allowing lenders to assess the risks. They set the price of the risk by setting the interest rate and down payment they require to loan money to the investment.

Misrepresenting (lying about) the investment's risk distorts the market's ability to price risk, and so does government guarantees to cover any losses suffered by the investors.

Imagine yourself in a casino where the owners will guarantee your losses up to $1 million. We call the disconnect of risk from loss "moral hazard," and to understand the ramifications of moral hazard, we compare the actions of two gamblers in the casino: one is using his own money, the other has none of his own money at risk, as his losses will be covered up to $1 million by the casino owners.

How much risk will you accept if you can lose $1 million without any loss to yourself? Obviously, we will accept enormous risks because if we win a high-risk bet, the gain will be ours to keep while any loss will be transferred to the casino owners. Since low-risk bets yield low returns and high-risk bets yield high returns, why bother with low-risk bets?

Once risk has been freed from consequence, then the incentives favor increasing risk at every opportunity.

If we actually win a few high-risk bets, this success feeds our risk appetite. Our wins reinforce our risk appetite, while losing bets no longer register in our minds: since someone else absorbs the loss, losses have been eliminated from our calculations of risk and gain.

This eventually leads us to make gigantic bets. Eventually, we bet $1 million on a high-risk play and lose. We are wiped out, but oh well, it was fun while it lasted.

The risk didn't disappear, of course; it was simply transferred to the casino owners who now have to absorb the $1 million loss.

Since the casino has many investors, the $1 million loss, catastrophic to any one player, is spread over a large group of people. As a result, the loss suffered by each investor is modest.

This is the key to understanding "moral hazard:" if the gains are kept by the gambler while the losses are spread over a large group, the losses aren't big enough to each investor to trigger their alarm. Nobody who loses $1,000 as an investor is going to say, "Hey, this thing is getting out of hand."

The potential for huge winnings motivates the gambler to keep making big, risky bets, while the modest size of each investor's share of the losses don't appear dangerous to the investors.

Let's say the casino didn't tell the whole truth about this "moral hazard" guarantee. If the casino told its investors, "This guy never loses, that's why we're covering his bets up to $1 million," the real risk was misrepresented. The casino's investors didn't protest because they were given false information about the real risks. Withholding or manipulating information transfers risk to every investor.

But let's suppose the player with the $1 million guarantee was extraordinarily successful with high-risk bets, and he built the $1 million stake into $100 million, which he then rolled into several giant bets.

He loses, because the risk of gambling hasn't been eliminated. Now the casino owners face a loss 100 times its guaranteed "maximum loss."

If the casino is worth $90 million, it too will be wiped out.

This is how one player who manages to transfer risk to others can bring down the entire system. The risk only appears manageable at the start, but since consequence has been eliminated from the players' perspective and spectacular gain is all that he experiences, the risk piles up.

Since the system itself has disconnected risk from consequence, it is has lost the feedback required to adapt to reality. On the surface, the player turning his initial $1 million stake into $100 million looks like he's doing good business for the casino. It's only when the last giant bet is lost that the casino realizes the true size of the risk, but it's too late: the casino and all its investors are wiped out.

In the real world, American taxpayers are like the casino investors. While the Wall Street financier gamblers were winning, it looked like we were winning, too. But when the bets got too big, we didn't grasp the risk to the system; so we let them keep gambling until they lost.

Since we guaranteed their losses, now we're wiped out, too.

There are two critically important things to understand here:

1. Everything was legal and above board. There was no fraud committed at the gaming tables or in the casino bankrolling the gambler.

2. People pursue the incentives (profits) that are offered and avoid disincentives (losses).

If you offer people "free money," they will pursue it.

If you make fraud easy and profitable, people will become liars and swindlers.

If you cover the losses of a gambler, they will gamble for higher stakes with bigger bets.

This is why things are falling apart: the Status Quo rewards moral hazard, misrepresenting the truth and speculation, and punishes saving, honesty and transparent pricing of risk.

If we leave these incentives in place, our children will inherit a hollowed-out, corrupt and thoroughly bankrupt economy and society.

As noted earlier, even if we got rid of all the fraud, manipulation, and white-collar crime that permeates our financial system, it wouldn't stop the system from falling apart. That's the key lesson of the casino example. If you guarantee speculators against loss, they will take risks that will eventually sink the entire economy. That's precisely what happened in 2008, and it will keep on happening until we let the banks and financiers fail when they lose speculative bets.

Understanding Debt: The Family That Borrows 40% of Its Budget

You may have seen the word "fractal" or the phrase "scale-invariant." They both describe things that look similar on a small and large scale. Nature often displays this characteristic. For example, a jagged coastline looks similar in a photo taken from an elevation of 100 feet, 1,000 feet and 10,000 feet. The scale changes but the characteristics remain similar.

Finance is the same way: its characteristics don't change as the scale changes. The finances of a household earning $38,000 a year, a corporation earning $380 million a year and a government that spends $3.8 trillion a year (the U.S. government) share the same features: interest must be paid on debt, income and expenses must balance or there is a deficit, and a balance sheet lists assets and liabilities.

Since finance is scale-invariant (the same at all scales), we can understand the national budget by looking at a household budget. In terms of accounting principles, there is no difference between the two. This is a key "building block" concept that helps us understand the entire economy by breaking it down into household examples.

Let's take a family that earns $30,000 a year but wants to consume (spend) $50,000. Their "solution" to the gap between what they earn and what they want to spend is to borrow $20,000 every year. That $20,000 is 40% of their entire budget.

Let's say the household has good credit and can borrow at 10% interest. To maximize the amount that can be spent, the household pays only the interest and nothing on the principal (the amount borrowed), so the family debt rises by $20,000 every year.

(To keep our example straightforward, we're using simple rather than compound interest.)

The first year, the family pays 10% of the $20,000 or $2,000 in interest. That leaves $18,000 of the borrowed $20,000 to spend.

The second year, the household borrows another $20,000, so the debt has doubled to $40,000 and the interest payment is $4,000. That leaves $16,000 of the borrowed $20,000 to spend.

The third year, the debt has tripled to $60,000, and the 10% interest comes to $6,000. That leaves $14,000 of the borrowed $20,000 to spend.

In the fourth year, the total amount borrowed has risen to $80,000, and the interest is now $8,000. That leaves $12,000 of the borrowed $20,000 to spend.

In the fifth year, the total debt has climbed to $100,000, and the interest is now $10,000. That leaves $10,000 of the borrowed $20,000 to spend.

The family is now borrowing $10,000 a year just to pay the interest.

In year six, the interest is $12,000, in year seven it rises to $14,000, and in year eight it totals $16,000, as the total debt has risen to $160,000. In year nine, the interest is $18,000, and in year ten the debt reaches $20,000: the interest consumes the entire $20,000 that's borrowed every year.

In year 11, the family not only has to borrow $20,000 just to pay the interest on its accumulated debt, it has to cut its other spending because the interest payment is $22,000—more than the family borrows every year.

In a few more years, the interest is $30,000 a year, and the family is much worse off than it was before it started borrowing 40% of its budget, because now it can only spend $20,000 of its $30,000 earnings: not only is the entire $20,000 that is borrowed going to interest, $10,000 of their other income is also devoted to paying interest.

Eventually, the family's entire earnings go to paying interest. There is nothing left to live on.

The U.S.A. is like this family. Since 2009, the U.S. government has borrowed around 40% of its budget each and every year. The Federal budget is about $3.8 trillion, and we're borrowing about $1.5 trillion each year. (Various accounting tricks are used to lower the "headline" deficit, but the real borrowing is higher than we're told. "Supplemental appropriations" is one of the tricks.)

The national debt (what's called "external debt") has almost doubled four short years later, and there is no end in sight.

The 'family" that is the U.S.A. refuses to live within its means, and refuses to spend only what it generates in surplus. It wants to spend, spend, spend, consume, consume, consume, and so it borrows gigantic sums every year.

Just like the family in our example, we're borrowing to pay the interest on our past borrowing. Soon, we'll be cutting other spending just to pay the interest. Eventually, most of our tax revenues will be spent on interest. All the other government programs people want will be trimmed because the first priority of any debtor is to pay the interest. If the borrower stops paying interest, nobody will lend them more money, and the whole "fool Mother Nature by borrowing money" game will end.

As mentioned before, people prefer denial because it's easier than facing unwelcome truths. People make excuses for falsehoods and offer all sorts of rationalizations and justifications. They will do anything to avoid facing the hard truth.

But we all know what happens when you sweep problems under the rug—they get worse. Debt is a problem that gets worse by its very nature, because the more you borrow the more income goes to pay interest.

Let's return to our household example. Let's say the family wants to keep spending $20,000 extra every year. Since interest has to be paid, the interest cuts the amount available to spend. In year one, the family has to spend $2,000 paying interest, so they only get to spend $18,000 of the $20,000 they borrowed that year.

Let's say they don't like sacrificing $2,000 of their borrowed money to pay interest. Their "solution" is to borrow the $20,000 they want to spend and then borrow enough to cover the interest. So in year one they borrow $22,200--$20,000 to spend (consume) and $2,200 to pay the 10% interest on the $22,000 debt.

If the family keeps borrowing enough to spend $20,000 "extra" and pay 10% interest on all the debt they're piling up, by year five they have to borrow $32,210; the total debt has ballooned to $134,312 and their interest payment is $12,210. In five short years, they are borrowing more than they earn each year to maintain their $50,000 a year spending.

By year ten, the interest payment has risen to $31,874 and total debt is $350,623. The family is now paying more in interest than they earn to spend the $20,000 each year they didn't earn.

If you know Excel or a similar spreadsheet program, you can quickly set up a simple-interest calculation like I did and confirm this astronomical rise in debt and interest.

In the real world, no bank would keep lending money to such a spendthrift household.

The U.S.A. is like this family. We want to keep spending more than we pay in taxes, more than the nation earns in surplus, and we also want to borrow enough that the interest payment doesn't crimp our spending.

This is a path straight to bankruptcy, and it's doesn't matter if it's a household, a company or a country: you can't borrow 40% of your budget and borrow the interest payment, too, for very long before "Mother Nature" catches up with you.

The U.S.A. has a central bank called the Federal Reserve (actually, a privately owned bank) that can artificially lower interest rates. If the U.S. can borrow money at low rates of interest, then we can "fool Mother Nature" for longer. But the end result is the same: in a few years, the interest payments will eat up most of the government's tax revenues.

Is this sustainable? We know it is not, and the losers will be future generations.

Why Can't We Just Print the Money We Want To Spend?

Many people say that we don't need to borrow money at all. If we want to spend more than we earn, all we need to do is print money.

But the problem with this idea is easily revealed. Expanding the supply of money does not expand the supply of real-world commodities, which are intrinsically limited. These include water, minerals and oil. The average household in the U.S. earns about $49,000 annually. If every household were given $1 million tomorrow in freshly printed dollars (20 times our income), it wouldn't create 20 times more oil. Prices would quickly rise so one hour of labor would buy the same amount of tangible goods that it bought before the $1 million expansion in our personal money supply.

Let's say I make $20 an hour and I can buy five gallons of gasoline with that $20 (gas is $4 per gallon). If everyone was suddenly paid 20 times more, and I made $400 an hour, then the price of gasoline would quickly adjust so my one hour of labor would still buy the same five gallons of gasoline.

The idea that we can "print our way to prosperity" is false, because printing money does not create more surplus. (Please refer back to our explanation of surplus: you can only spend what you make in surplus.) Since we cannot "print" oil, labor, wheat, water or steel, then printing money doesn't "fool Mother Nature."

Forty-five years ago in 1966, few would have believed a prediction that the auto that cost $3,000 in 1966 would cost $30,000 in the future and a small apartment that rented for $120 a month would cost $1,200 a month. Yet that is what has happened. Expanding the supply of money does not expand the supply of tangible goods, so prices rise to match the increase in printed money.

The more rapid the expansion of credit and money, the more rapid the price increases to match. In other words, if we were all given $1 trillion tomorrow, our ability to buy tangible goods would not change much, as prices would quickly jump to the point that it would still take 40 hours of labor to pay a month's rent, or an hour of labor to buy four loaves of bread, six hours to buy a barrel of oil, and so on. The purchasing power of our money would be unchanged, despite the many zeroes added to our money. The only real measure of money is how many tangible goods can be purchased with it, and we can only spend what we've created in surplus.

Borrowing money that will never be paid back is trying to get "something for nothing." Printing money is just another form of "something for nothing." Both are attempts to "fool Mother Nature," and both fail.

The Federal Reserve and "Free Money"

America's central bank is called the Federal Reserve, and it is not a government agency, it is a privately owned bank that was given special powers by Congress at its founding in 1913. (The Fed is owned by a consortium of private banks.) Its official purpose is to "smooth out" the business cycle of expansion and contraction so recessions (contraction of credit and the economy) are shallow and brief. Its other job is to keep prices and employment stable.

But behind these lofty sounding goals, the Fed's real purpose is supporting and enriching banks and financiers.

Common sense tells us there are two ways a household can borrow more money: one is the household earns more money. If you earn an extra $100 a month that could be spent on a loan payment, you can borrow $1,000. We say the $100 per month "leverages" the $1,000 loan: each $1 of income enables $10 in debt.

Lenders loan money based on the amount of income available to pay the debt: the more income available to pay principal and interest, the more money the bank will lend. If you want to borrow more money, you need to earn more income.

There is another way to borrow more, however: lower the interest rate of the loan. If $100 leverages a $1,000 loan at 10% interest, then it will leverage $2,000 at 5% interest and $4,000 at 2.5% interest.

Notice how the "magic" of low interest rates works: if you drop the interest rate enough, a small income can suddenly support a very large loan.

This is how people with modest incomes were able to buy $400,000 homes in the housing bubble. They bought the home with no money down, and the "teaser" interest rate was very low.

Now imagine if you could borrow money at 0% interest. You could borrow $1 million "interest only," and pay absolutely nothing every month. The $1 million would truly be "free money" because you don't have to pay any interest at all.

What would you do with $1 million in "free money"? One thing you could do is loan it to somebody willing to pay 5% interest. You would then be earning $50,000 a year on your free money, $50,000 that you didn't have to earn. Wouldn't that be great?

Now imagine if you could borrow $1 billion at 0% interest, and loan it out at 10%. You would earn $100 million a year in interest, with no expenses because your interest payment for the $1 billion was zero. Wouldn't that be great?

This is precisely what the Federal Reserve offers banks: it gives them 0% loans and the banks then loan the "free money" out and collect billions of dollars in interest.

Is your credit card 0% interest (after the "teaser rate" expires)? No. It might be 9.9%, or 19%. Is your student loan 0%? No, it might be 6% or 9%.

How much interest do you earn on your savings? Less than zero, if we adjust for inflation.

Now you understand how our financial system is rigged to benefit the banks and financiers, and how it skims hard-earned money from the productive many and diverts it to the unproductive, parasitic few. What did the bankers do to earn these billions in interest? Nothing: the reason they earn billions is the Federal Reserve gave them free money at 0% interest. Anyone could make $1 billion in interest if they received $10 billion in free money at 0% interest.

Where does the Federal Reserve get all this money? It creates it with a keystroke on a computer, conjuring it out of thin air. We say the Fed "prints" the money but it doesn't actually print money—it creates it electronically, and then "loans" it to banks at 0% or buys assets with it.

The rest of us need collateral or income to borrow money, but the banks don't need anything to borrow billions; they have the Federal Reserve to hand then free money in nearly unlimited quantities.

If we look at the Fed's actions and policies rather than their words, their guiding motto is "We take from the poor and give to the super-rich." The Fed is truly Robin Hood in reverse, and ultimately it's our children who will be paying interest on debt we accumulated for their entire lives.

Few people think that the "Reverse Robin Hood" Federal Reserve is a threat to their children, but if an Empire conquered America and turned our children into impoverished debt-serfs, wouldn't you consider that a threat? This is the value of official propaganda and marketing: the direct threat to our children's future posed by ever-rising debt is so well obscured most people don't even see it.

As long as the Federal Reserve exists, the banks have guaranteed profits which they can use to buy political influence and control. The Federal Reserve and our dependence on debt have ceded control of our economy and government to a feudal oligarchy of financiers. Our children are the losers.

Understanding Leverage

There are two kinds of debt, secured and unsecured. We secure a debt with collateral: we offer the lender something of value so if we default on the loan, they have something they can sell to recover the money they loaned to us.

A pawn shop, for example, would accept a diamond ring as collateral for a loan they make. If the owner didn't pay the loan back, the shop would sell the diamond ring to recover the loan amount.

Unsecured debt is a loan that is secured by future income rather than a valuable object. A credit card is essentially an unsecured loan: you borrow money from the bank when you charge a purchase. When you apply for a credit card, the bank wants to know about your income and other debt payments, because the credit account will be secured by your future income. People with very little income left after deducting other loan payments are considered poor credit risks, because they don't have enough income to pay additional debt.

A key characteristic of debt is leverage, which is scale-invariant, meaning that it works the same for individuals, corporations and nations. If collateral supports a loan that is much larger than the collateral's value, that's called leverage.

We can visualize leverage as a seesaw: when there is no leverage, the seesaw is level. For example, if we pawn a diamond ring worth $1,000 and receive a loan for $1,000, there is no leverage: the loan is 100% secured by the collateral.

In a traditional home mortgage, the buyer offers 20% in cash as a down payment: that's the collateral for the loan. The other 80% of the mortgage is unsecured, that is, based on future income. In this case, the collateral (the cash down payment) is only 20% of the value of the loan, so the leverage is 1-to-4: every dollar of cash supports $4 of debt. To buy a $100,000 home, the buyer puts down $20,000, which is the collateral for an $80,000 mortgage.

The seesaw is now tilted, as the bank has accepted $1 in collateral for every $4 of loaned money. If the buyer defaults on the mortgage, they forfeit their $20,000. The bank is also at risk: if the bank sells the house for $60,000, it loses $20,000 of its $80,000 mortgage.

Leverage is risky for the lender when the collateral is small. For example, a home buyer with an FHA mortgage may put only 3% in cash as the down payment. In this case, the seesaw is pointed at the sky, as every dollar in cash collateral supports $32 in debt.

If the buyer defaults, the bank will lose money is the house sells for less than 97% of the purchase price. The collateral is razor-thin.

So far we've been looking at leverage from the point of view of the borrower. But there is also leverage in the way banks originate loans.

In a traditional setting, the bank accepts $100 in cash deposits, and sets aside $10 in reserve to pay back depositors who come in and want to withdraw their savings. That leaves $90 for the bank to loan. The interest earned on the $90 is the bank's income.

The U.S. has what's known as a fractional reserve banking system: the bank's reserves are a mere fraction of the loans it has originated. In a fractional reserve banking system, a $20 loan is supported by $1 in cash. If the bank has $100 in cash deposits, it sets aside $2 in reserve to pay back depositors and then leverages the remaining $98 in cash into new loans at 20-to-1 leverage. The bank can issue a loan for $1,960 with the $98 as the only collateral.

High leverage is extremely dangerous should assets decline in value or debtors default on loans. For example, let's say the bank issued a mortgage of $100,000 to buy a house that cost $103,000 (the buyer only put down 3% in cash). At 20-to-1 leverage, the bank has $5,000 in cash supporting the $100,000 loan. If the buyer defaults and the house is sold for $90,000, the bank has lost its entire $5,000 collateral and another $5,000 it doesn't even have. The bank is insolvent, meaning that the bank's liabilities exceed its assets. It is bankrupt, and has to close.

In a fractional reserve banking system, the bank only has to keep 2% of deposits in cash. As soon as the rumor of insolvency hits, depositors rush to withdraw their money. Only the first 2% of deposits can be paid, and then the bank closes its doors. The other 98% is lost and cannot be recovered.

This is what happened in the Great Depression: not only were the banks wiped out, so were the savers who had entrusted their cash with the banks.

Nowadays, savings accounts are insured by the Federal government up to $250,000, so if a bank closes down, only those people with more than $250,000 in the bank lose money.

I hope these examples reveal the extreme danger of highly leveraged loans, mortgages and banks. A very slight loss brings down the entire system.

In broad brush, that's the problem with America's financial system: high leverage has made it extremely vulnerable to collapse, as modest losses quickly wipe out all the collateral supporting loans.

You now see the appeal of high leverage. When leverage was 1-to-1, and the bank could only loan out the $90 it had in cash deposits, the bank's profits were limited. With 20-to-1 leverage, the bank can make 20 times the profit.

Although it is beyond the scope of this book, there are financial instruments called derivatives that enable the bank to increase its leverage far beyond 20-to-1. This means the slightest loss will bankrupt the bank. This is what triggered the 2008 global financial meltdown, and the European debt crisis.

Borrowers have also feasted on dangerous leverage, leveraging small 3% down payments 32-to-1 and exaggerating income to obtain mortgages that are beyond their means. The slightest decline in housing prices or income bankrupts the over-leveraged household just like it bankrupts the over-leveraged bank.

It's important to understand that high leverage creates risks that are quite different from the risks we learned about in the casino example.

Let's return to the mortgage example, but this time the borrower has a no-down, "no-document" mortgage. Let's say the actual cash the buyer puts up is $1,000. That $1,000 is leveraging a $100,000 loan. That's 100-to-1 leverage.

Since the borrower's income and employment isn't verified, the bank has nothing for collateral except the house itself. A loan without collateral is very high risk. If the borrower defaults, the bank forecloses the house. If the bank sells the house for $100,000, the transaction and legal fees will take at roughly 10% of the home's sales price. The bank will lose money unless the home rose in value.

The borrower has essentially no "skin in the game." He could buy the house as a speculative bet, and lose very little if the bet doesn't pan out. Once people see others buying and "flipping" houses purchased with no-down payment loans, they pile into the same speculation.

As I said earlier: people will pursue whatever incentives the system offers. In the housing bubble, buying a house with a no-document, no-down loan and then selling it a few months later for a fat profit was very rewarding, while the potential loss was limited to a few thousand dollars in closing costs.

Banks had the same incentives to increase speculation and ignore the basic rules of risk management: the profits generated by extreme leverage were simply too enormous to pass up.

Low risk, potentially high gain: it was a very appealing speculation to both lender and borrower.

If everyone in town bought homes with no collateral, two things happen as borrowers default: banks start failing as their losses mount, and home prices plummet as lenders unload their foreclosed houses. That sets up a feedback loop: the more houses banks put on the market, the more prices decline, and the bigger the losses the banks must absorb.

Leverage creates risks in a number of ways. Let's say a bank wants to lend more money to generate more profit, but its deposits aren't growing. Rather than create credit at 25-to-1 leverage, it increases the leverage to 50-to-1. It can now double the size of its loan portfolio, and double its profits.

But at 50-to-1 leverage, there is only $2 of cash for every $100 of outstanding loans. If one loan goes bad (the borrower defaults) and the bank loses $2, its reserves are wiped out. If it loses $3, it is insolvent: it owes more than it owns in assets.

This is the problem with leverage: it increases the risk of cascading insolvencies in lenders, borrowers, and ultimately, the financial system itself.

Leverage works the same way for banks, households and whole economies: a small amount of collateral supports an enormous pile of debt. The entire global economy now depends on leverage not just for its growth but for its very survival.

Now that the global housing bubble has deflated and prices have declined substantially, there is no collateral left to support the mountain of debt. Debt that is supposed to be secured is actually unsecured, although nobody dares admit this.

The banks are listing a mortgaged house at $100,000 on their books when in reality the house is only worth $80,000. Why? To avoid having to admit there is no collateral left to support the mortgage. If the bank admitted the collateral is gone, it would have to declare bankruptcy.

The banks are now so over-leveraged, so big and so politically powerful that they can hold the government hostage: banks are in effect saying, "Don't you dare let us go bankrupt, because if you do we'll take down the entire financial system." Banks have become so powerful that they are extorting endless bailouts from the Federal government and Federal Reserve.

By some estimates, these bailouts, subsidies, tax loopholes and guarantees total around $23 trillion, more than the value of all residential real estate in the U.S. Ultimately, all this bailout money is paid by taxpayers and future taxpayers—our children and grandchildren.

Politicians are fond of repeating the lie that "debt doesn't matter," but we now see that debt and leverage do matter. All unsecured debt is based on future income, and for the Federal government that means future tax revenue. Politicians always assume tax revenues will rise to the sky, allowing the government to easily pay its rising interest on its ballooning debt.

But what if tax revenues decline as the economy stagnates? Imagine a two-wage earner household with a big mortgage payment to make every month. What happens if one wage earner loses their job or has their hours cut? When income goes down, the debt becomes much harder to pay.

Now imagine the household is borrowing 40% of its budget every year. That means its debt payments keep getting larger each and every year. If the household income drops, it becomes impossible to keep paying the ever-higher interest payments. The household has no choice but to default, that is, stop paying all its bills.

The U.S. is like this family. Many people claim it is "impossible" for the Federal government to default on its debt because it can "print as much money as it needs." But this isn't true, for the simple reason that the government doesn't print money into existence—the Federal Reserve creates money electronically. The Federal Reserve is not a government agency, so the government doesn't get the "free money" created by the Federal Reserve. The Federal government has to borrow the money it wants to spend, and that borrowed money accrues interest that must be paid by taxpayers.

If any entity, household, business or government, keeps borrowing huge sums of money every year while its income stays flat, eventually the interest accruing on all that ever-rising debt eats up most of the income. There is no way around this simple reality.

Leverage and Interest Rates

Lenders charge interest on loans (debt), and those interest payments are claims on future earnings. The earnings of the borrower are the collateral for the loan, especially if it is consumer debt or student loans, where there is no collateral pledged to back the loan.

It's important to understand that any loan is leveraging the future income of the borrower.

We can understand this by returning to the home mortgage example. Let's say a household has $12,000 in its annual budget to spend on housing. If the interest rate for mortgages is 15% (as it was in 1981), the household can only qualify for a $50,000 mortgage. That's all the debt that can be prudently leveraged from the $12,000 in income devoted to housing.

In an economy that depends on debt-based spending for its growth, and on higher leverage to increase the amount of debt that can originated and borrowed, the interest rate is a key factor.

In an open market economy, the "price" of borrowing money is the interest rate. The interest rate is set by supply and demand: how much cash has been deposited in banks, how much savers demand in interest for their savings, how much borrowers are willing to pay, and the profit margin the banks demand.

All of these factors interact in the marketplace to set the interest rate paid to savers and the rate borrowers must pay. The difference between the two rates is the bank's earnings for managing the deposits and originating loans.

When the government and central bank start managing the economy they soon realize that the interest rate sets the leverage on borrowers' future income. If they lower the interest rate, every $1 in income can support a lot more debt.

For example, suppose the central bank intervenes in the market and drops the mortgage rate to 1%. As if by magic, the household with $12,000 annually to spend on housing now "qualifies" for a $500,000 mortgage. When interest rates were high (and rewarding savers), the household's income could only be leveraged 4-to-1; they could only qualify for a $50,000 mortgage.

When interest rates are near-zero, that same household now qualifies for a $500,000 mortgage at 42-to-1 leverage.

This greatly increases the leverage and thus the risk in the financial system.

You might see the problem low interest rates create: once rates fall to near-zero, the leverage-income-into-more-debt machine runs out of room. Once rates are near-zero, there's no more leverage to be had. The "increase leverage to increase debt" game is over.

That's where America is today: interest rates are near-zero, and there's no more leverage to be squeezed out of lowering interest rates. An economy dependent on ever-increasing debt and leverage is running on fumes and will soon sputter to a halt.

Playing Games with Collateral and Phantom Assets

Banks are regulated by the Federal government and the Federal Reserve, America's privately owned central bank. Once leverage has reached high levels, the amount of collateral (reserves) held by the bank is razor-thin. At 25-to-1 leverage, if only 3% of the bank's portfolio of loans go bust, the bank's reserves are wiped out and the bank is insolvent.

Since the banks' managers and owners are wealthy and politically connected, the government steps in to keep them from going bust. The government has two tricks it can play to make insolvent banks look healthy:

1) It can lower the reserve requirements
2) It can allow the bank to pledge phantom assets as collateral

We've already seen how lowering the reserve against losses works. If the government lowers the bank reserve requirement from 2% to 1%, it has given the bank permission to double the size of its loan portfolio.

Suppose the bank reserve requirement is 2% of all outstanding loans. If the bank has lost 1% of its loan portfolio, its reserve is now 1%. It no longer meets reserve requirements, and must raise capital (cash) to bring reserves back up to 2%.

Or the government can lower the reserve requirement to 1%, and save the bank the trouble of raising cash. There are other tricks the central bank and government play to keep politically powerful banks from going bust, but they're too complex to describe in this short book.

One that we can all understand is allowing the banks to pledge phantom assets as collateral that backs up the banks' loans.

Suppose a bank owns a luxury condominium in Florida because the owner defaulted on the mortgage. The condo was originally sold for $300,000, but the market value of the condo is now $100,000. The mortgage was $250,000. If the bank sold the condo, it would have to absorb a $150,000 loss. ($250,000 - $100,000 = $150,000)

Instead of absorbing a loss that might push the bank into insolvency, the bank's solution is to keep the condo on its balance sheet as being worth $300,000. Not only does the loss go away, the bank actually has $50,000 of assets which it can leverage into $1 million in new loans. ($300,000 asset - $250,000 mortgage = $50,000 in collateral; at 20-to-1 leverage, that $50,000 leverages $1 million in new loans.)

The $50,000 in collateral is a phantom asset. Not only does it misrepresent the bank's real collateral; it is increasing the leverage and risk in the entire system.

Once the government allows lenders to increase leverage and play games with phantom assets and collateral, the entire system is at risk of domino-like insolvencies.

Money and Credit

We think we understand money, but it's actually a complex topic.

We could read dozens of textbooks and hundreds of articles about it, but it boils down to some simple basics.

Money is two things: it is a means of exchange and it is a store of value.

Anything can become a means of exchange: shells, salt, gold, silver, paper with symbols printed on it, etc. In the past, it tended to be whatever was rare (salt and shells were "money" in mountains far from the sea, for example) and what was durable (gold and silver).

Before the Spanish and Portuguese began shipping huge quantities of gold and silver from their conquered territories in Latin America, there was a shortage of gold and silver coinage in Europe. There simply wasn't enough money to facilitate expanding trade. In Medieval trade fairs, paper bills of exchange lubricated global trade. Here's how it worked: I give you a paper credit for the tea I bought from you, and you give me a similar note for the cotton you bought from me.

The tea is worth $1,000 and the cotton is worth $990. The difference is $10, which I pay you with a silver coin.

So the "real money" exchanged for $1,990 worth of traded goods was $10. The amount of credit is more important than the amount of cash money. A mere $10 in cash money greased an exchange of value of $1,990.

This example illustrates the critical role of credit in trade. The essential ingredient in credit is trust. There is no intrinsic value in the paper notes we exchanged; it was a trade based on transparency (we could inspect the tea and cotton independently, and "discover" the price by shopping around the open-market fair) and trust: we have to trust that the other one isn't perpetrating some kind of fraud.

Once trust is lost due to fraud or dishonesty, credit and trade both disappear. Since trade is a key engine of wealth creation, the economy becomes poorer if trust is destroyed.

It's very important to understand the difference between a trade credit and a loan. Credit issued to conduct business must be settled in a short period time: by the end of the fair, the end of the month, etc.

A loan is credit that is extended for a set amount of money for a set amount of time. It is loaned at interest, meaning that it must be paid back with interest. Examples include auto loans, home mortgages and student loans.

Money Velocity and "Dead Money"

A story made the rounds on the Web a few years ago in which a single $100 bill is passed from debtor to debtor in a small town. By the time it passes through everyone's hands, the single $100 has erased the entire town's debts.

This is a good example of what is called the velocity of money—how "fast" it travels through the real economy. In the Web story, a single $100 bill passed from creditor to debtor again and again, until everyone's debts to another town resident were paid. This $100 bill flowed quickly and positively through the town's economy. It had a high velocity.

For an example of zero velocity, let's say every household and business in town each put $100 in the town bank. The bank decided to keep high reserves because business conditions were poor, and when the bank tried to lend the cash, there were no takers: nobody wanted any more debt or another loan.

All that cash sits in the bank vault, going nowhere. Its velocity is zero.

"Dead money" has low velocity. Productive money has high velocity.

There are all sorts of ways money can become "dead money," unable to enter the real economy.

One example is a household "owning more house than it can afford." Let's say a household could have bought a house with a $1,000 per month mortgage but instead bought a much larger house with a $2,000 per month mortgage. If that house has lost value, the household isn't building equity with their extra $1,000 a month payment; the money is vanishing down a black hole. It's dead money to the household.

The household could have done something else with that $1,000 per month; it could have consumed it or invested it. What could have been done with that money is called the "opportunity cost" that was lost in the decision to buy more house than the household could afford.

It's important to understand money velocity, because it explains why the Federal Reserve (America's privately owned central bank) can electronically "print" $1 trillion and give it to the banks at 0% interest, and none of it flows into the real economy. The banks, having lost billions in imprudent mortgages and speculative bets, have very low reserves. So they hold on to the money as reserves.

Potential borrowers have little interest in taking on more debt in an erratic economy.

So the $1 trillion in money sits in reserves. The Federal Reserve wants the banks to push it into the real economy, but you can't force people to borrow money, especially if their incomes and assets have declined.

You can print $1 trillion, but if it sits in reserves then it is dead money.

If the money is invested in houses nobody wants or can afford, or factories that make things nobody wants, the money is called "stranded capital," as it was stranded in an unproductive place. This is another way of saying "dead money" that can no longer enter the real economy.

I will end with a story about economic history that beautifully illustrates dead money and money velocity.

In the Medieval and Renaissance eras, there was a brisk global trade between Europe, the Mideast and Asia via great fleets of sailing ships plying the seas and caravans traveling over the long land routes of the Silk Road to China. The rulers of India and China considered gold and silver the only "real money," so they demanded gold or silver for their silk, spices and other goods.

The capitalist Western Europe expanded its wealth via trade with the East. It invested its trading profits in ships, harbors, canals and networks of suppliers and traders. It extended credit and traded stocks and insurance policies.

The rulers of China and India kept their gold and silver in vaults. It was dead money, with zero velocity. It wasn't invested in productive enterprises or infrastructure, and so the wealth of the East was unproductive.

As a result, the Western European trading powers overtook the great Asian empires and came to dominate global trade. This is why India and China, which were much wealthier and had much larger economies than Europe in 1350, were bypassed by Europe and America.

There are many political and cultural reasons for Asia being eclipsed, but the failure to invest wealth productively is a key economic reason.

Squandering wealth on excessive consumption and malinvestment or burying it in "dead money" vaults leads to widespread poverty and decline.

Understanding Inflation and Deflation

The conventional view is that inflation is good and deflation is bad. The truth is that inflation is good for banks and bad for households, while deflation is bad for banks and good for households.

Since ours is a bank credit system enforced by the Central State, what's bad for the banks is presumed to be bad for everyone.

This is simply not true. Inflation is "good" for borrowers, but only if their income rises while their debts remain fixed. For everyone with stagnant income, inflation is just officially sanctioned theft.

The conventional view can be illustrated with this example. Let's say a household earns $50,000 a year and they have a fixed-rate mortgage of $100,000. If they set aside 40% of their income to pay the mortgage, that's $20,000 a year. This means they can pay off their mortgage in five years. (To keep things simple, let's ignore interest.)

Let's say the household's annual grocery bill is $5,000—10% of the annual income.

If inflation causes all prices and incomes to double, the household income rises to $100,000 and groceries cost $10,000—still 10% of the annual income. In this sense, inflation hasn't changed anything: it still takes the same number of hours of work to buy the household's groceries.

But inflation does something magical when incomes rise and debts remain fixed: now 40% of the household income is $40,000, and so the household can pay off the fixed-rate mortgage in only two-and-a-half years.

Why is inflation good for the banks? After all, the mortgage is paid with depreciated money that no longer buys what it used to. Inflation benefits the banks for the simple reason that it enables the household to make its debt payments *and borrow more*.

Remember that banks don't just earn profits on interest, they make money on transaction fees: issuing loans and processing payments. The more loans they originate and manage, the more money they make. The more debt and leverage increase, the more money the banks make.

Banks don't actually hold many of the loans they originate. They bundle the loans and sell them to investors, a process called securitization. The banks bundle the loans into a security such as a mortgage-backed security (MBS) that can be sold in pieces to investors around the world.

The bank made its money when it originated the loan. Future inflation hurts the investors who bought the loan, not the bank. The bank sold the loan and booked the profit. To make more money, it needs to originate more loans. And to do that, it needs consumers who feel richer because inflation has boosted their nominal (face value) income.

It's all an illusion, of course; it still takes the same number of hours of labor to buy groceries. But this illusion of having a higher income encourages households to borrow more. This is how inflation greatly benefits banks.

But the mechanism falls apart if incomes don't rise along with prices for goods and services. When incomes stay the same and prices of goods and services rise, the household is poorer—their income buys less than it did before.

The mechanism also falls apart if interest rates rise while income stays flat. In adjustable rate loans and credit cards, for example, the interest rate can adjust higher; the rate is not fixed.

This is the situation we find ourselves in: 90% of households are experiencing stagnant or declining income, even as inflation raises the cost of goods and services every year. Major expenses like medical insurance and college tuition have been rising at 5% to 6% a year for decades, twice the official rate of inflation.

The Federal Reserve's policies are explicitly intended to create 3% inflation, as inflation benefits the banks. But since wages and incomes are not rising or even declining for 90% of households, the Fed's policy is stealing purchasing power from households and enriching the banks. The Fed is a "reverse Robin Hood," stealing from the poor to give to the rich.

Since we've been brainwashed into uncritically believing deflation is bad, we haven't thought it out for ourselves. Take computers as an example: the cost of computers and memory are dropping all the time. Our money buys more memory and computer power every year for less money. The cost of computers has deflated for decades. Calculated in 2012 dollars, I paid $5,350 for my first Macintosh computer in 1985. Last year I bought a Hewlett-Packard PC for $450, less than 10% of the cost of a computer in 1985, and the PC has 1,000 times the power and memory of a 1985-era computer.

This is deflation in action: our money buys more goods and services every year. How is this bad?

Not only is deflation good for the household with fixed or declining income, it's also good for the overall economy. How many people could afford a computer in 1985? Very few. How many can afford a computer now that they cost one-tenth as much? Almost everyone can afford one, even those households that are officially near the poverty line ($23,000 for a family of four in 2012).

If inflation had driven up the cost of computers while income stayed flat, even fewer people could afford computers, and manufacturers would have a much smaller market.

It's important to remember that adjusted for inflation, the median income for the lower 90% of wage earners (138 million people) has been flat since 1970—forty years. Only the top 10% (14 million people) actually gained income, and only the top 5% gained significantly (+90%). The only way 90% of the populace can buy more goods and services is with deflation.

Let's consider a household that earns $1,000 a month that enables them to buy 100 good and services. At 4% inflation, in five years the household will only be able to afford 80 goods and services, because inflation stole 20% of the value (purchasing power) of their money. Those producing and selling goods and services have lost 20% of their market.

At 4% deflation, in five years they can afford 120 goods and services—20% more. If you are producing a good or service, your market has expanded by 20%.

Let's total the consequences of inflation and deflation. With 4% inflation, households are poorer, as they can buy fewer goods and services, and those producing goods and services see their market shrink by 20%. Inflation is a disaster for everyone but the banks.

With deflation, households' purchasing power increases by 20% and the market for goods and services also increases by 20%. If productivity rises more than 20% over five years, companies can actually produce and sell 20% more goods and make more profit than they did five years before.

What the banks and their servant the Federal Reserve want is for households to become poorer but more heavily indebted. They don't want households to be able to afford more goods and services—they want households to have to borrow more money to buy more goods and services because issuing more loans is how banks make huge profits.

Politicians love bank profits as much as the banks because they collect tens of millions of dollars in contributions (in more honest terms, bribes) from the banks. Politicians don't care if 90% of American households get poorer every year thanks to inflation created by the Federal Reserve: the 1/10th of 1% live in a completely separate world than the 99.9%.

The banks and their politician partners love inflation because it lines their pockets with tens of millions of dollars in profit. They have worked very hard to convince the 99.9% that inflation is good and deflation is bad, but it's simply not true. Inflation is a slow, continual theft that robs the working productive members of society and transfers the wealth to the banks and their cronies, the politicians and lobbyists.

Banks and the Federal Reserve hate deflation because people can buy more goods and services without borrowing money to do so.

If the bank and Federal Reserve's nightmare comes true and deflation occurs, something else happens that the banks hate: marginal borrowers default on all their debts. Rather than being easier to pay, the debts become more difficult to pay as money gains value. Marginal borrowers no longer get the "boost" of inflation, so they increasingly default on their loans.

The banks have to absorb the losses, and since they are so highly leveraged, the losses drive the banks into insolvency. They are bankrupt and must close their doors.

Once again 99.9% of the people benefit when bad banks absorb losses and have to close. Only the bank management, owners and bond holders lose, and everyone else gains as an unproductive, poorly managed bank no longer burdens the economy with its malinvestments and risky bets.

The Federal Reserve's policy of protecting the wealth and power of the banks while stealing from wage earners via inflation is a catastrophe for the nation and the 99.9% who are not financiers, politicians and lobbyists.

Summary: The Destructive Forces of Financialization

In the introduction, I listed five core reasons why things are falling apart:
1. Debt and financialization
2. Crony capitalism and the elimination of risk and consequence
3. Diminishing returns
4. Centralization

5. Technological, financial and demographic changes in our economy

Having reached the end of Section One, we now have all the key "building block" concepts to understand financialization: the dominance of extreme leverage and debt in our economy and the resulting political dominance of finance. We now understand why dependence on ever-expanding debt and leverage leads to malinvestment and crony capitalism, which then lead to the elimination of risk and accountability. These systemic inefficiencies lead to unproductive friction, speculation and "dead money" sinkholes that squander the limited surplus generated by our economy.

In relying on borrowed money to fund our consumption and investments, we have institutionalized diminishing returns: the more we borrow, the less we get in return on our investment. We have crossed the point of no return: every additional $1 of debt returns less than $1 in economic activity.

By squandering our limited surplus on unproductive uses and interest on rapidly expanding debt, the nation is eating its seed corn and indenturing future generations to pay debts that can never be paid off. We are spiraling down a "black hole" of ever-expanding debt and diminishing returns.

These are structural, systemic realities. They are not the result of a "few bad eggs" or one political party or the other being in power. They are the result of our entire system, not a few people or a few policies. The rot of financialization is destroying the very core of our economy and society, and laying waste to the future we will leave our children.

We covered the Federal Reserve's key role in financialization and crony capitalism in Section One. But there are other "building block" concepts we need to fully understand the Central Government's role in institutionalizing the destructive forces of financialization, crony capitalism and diminishing returns. We will cover these concepts in Section Two.

Section Two:
The Government, Manager of the Economy

Since government now dominates our economy and society, as things fall apart we need to understand its role as the manager of both finance and society.

There are three key "building block" concepts here:

1. The unprecedented level of control the Central State has gained over the economy and society

2. The failure of "central planning"

3. The negative consequences of extreme concentrations of wealth and power

These three concepts are related: central control requires concentrating power in the government. Concentrations of private wealth gain influence over the machinery of the State, which is directed to serve the interests of powerful Elites.

These Elites try to manage our complex economy "from the top down." This is called central planning, as a handful of people at the top of extreme concentrations of power (such as the Federal Reserve) control the levers of the economy.

Central planning can only occur if the government has gained power over the entire economy and society. Central planning is a key feature of totalitarian and Communist regimes because the government controls the economy and society.

To understand why central planning has failed and why it will always fail, we will turn to Nature and systems analysis for examples.

We must also understand how concentrated wealth inevitably captures the government's regulatory and financial agencies. Once the government has concentrated power into a few hands, this power acts like a magnet for everyone seeking to increase their own wealth by influencing government policy. Concentrations of political power attract concentrations of wealth which then buys influence over policy and regulation.

Lastly, we need to understand how the "immune system" that's supposed to limit the power of government has failed, allowing the State's power to grow like cancer.

Once again, the reasons why things are falling apart are structural; they are not caused by a few bad policies or white-collar criminals. They are problems with the system, not individuals in the system.

Government Is a Claim on National Income

A government is only possible in economies that generate enough surpluses to afford a government. Hunter-gatherer groups do not have formal governments because they don't generate enough surpluses to support one.

Thus all governments are basically claims on the national income. All government debt is a claim on future income of the citizens.

If the national income declines, then government must shrink. If government claims on future citizen incomes exceed those incomes, the government debt will be too large to support and it will collapse.

The point is that government can only expand if the national income is expanding. If income shrinks, government must shrink. By borrowing vast sums of money, we are staking enormous claims on our children's income. Those claims will impoverish our children and grandchildren, or they will be renounced—they will not be paid back, and the interest will not be paid.

Expanding debt allows the government to expand even if the national income declines. This is not sustainable for long: government is a claim on national income, and it can only expand if national surpluses are expanding. Once surplus declines, government must shrink accordingly. Filling the gap with trillions of dollars in borrowed money only guarantees future national bankruptcy.

The government must shrink as the economy stagnates and contracts. We can put this off for five years, or perhaps ten years, but eventually reality will impose a default "solution": the government will go bankrupt and repudiate all its debt.

The Three Elements of the Economy and Society

The economy and society are composed of three interwoven elements: community, the marketplace and government.

If you share a meal you've prepared with your neighbor, this is community. No money was exchanged and the government had no say over the meal. The transaction was not financial, it was social, and the government didn't regulate or control it.

If you open a lunch cart and sell your neighbor a meal, this is the marketplace. The meal has a "market value" set by supply and demand.

If your neighbor's meal is delivered and paid for by a governmental agency, that's the government.

The government also regulates various aspects of the marketplace: there are food safety regulations, the cart must be located in a designated place, taxes must be paid by buyer and seller and the transaction is made with legal tender (i.e. "Federal Reserve notes"—our paper dollars).

Community and the marketplace are generally dynamic and self-regulating; they exist in places where the government's only role is to protect people from criminals and fraud. They tend to arise spontaneously in all human societies. The transactions between people in the community and marketplace are voluntary, and millions of transactions occur without micro-managing by some higher authority (central planning).

Government is different; it operates according to rules, regulations and operational guidelines. It changes by "top down" orders from its managers or by consensus, such as elections or council meetings.

Community and the marketplace are self-organizing as individuals voluntarily trade goods and services or join groups such as churches, co-operatives, enterprises or corporations.

If any group consolidates enough power, it can gain control over the community and marketplace. If a corporation buys or bankrupts all its competitors, it becomes a monopoly which can set the price of its products and exploit its power. If a church consolidates enough power, it can take over the government and grant special benefits to its membership. If a clan gains military power, it can force obedience to its warlord.

Government consolidates and concentrates control in a hierarchical bureaucracy that has coercive power over the citizenry. If you don't obey the government's commands, the government can arrest and imprison you.

What enables coercion and exploitation is the concentration of power. If power remains diffused, it cannot easily become coercive.

Ideally, the three elements of society balance each other in equilibrium where no one element is able to concentrate enough power to dominate the economy and society. In the modern era, the Central State has gained dominance over society and the economy. Though we differentiate between Communist, Socialist and Capitalist systems, the unifying factor in all three systems is that the Central State dominates the society and economy.

The Government's Compromised "Immune System"

Clearly, a government's power can easily expand into dictatorship, for it holds the unique power of coercion. There are many words to describe this concentration of power into the hands of a few: plutocracy, oligarchy, theocracy, autocracy, tyranny, monarchy, despotism and totalitarianism.

The United States was founded on the principle that all government is prone to concentrating power and so the primary purpose of the Constitution is to limit the State's power and the power of those at the top of the government's bureaucracies.

The Founding Fathers attempted to limit government by separating it into three equally powerful branches of government: the Executive branch (the Presidency and cabinet agencies), the legislative branch (Congress) and the Judicial branch (the Supreme Court and Federal courts). The election process was intended to enable the citizens to choose their leadership, and the judiciary was intended to weed out any illegal power grabs that were attempted by either appointed or elected officials.

The system was intended to operate much like the immune system in the human body: when a threat arises, the government is supposed to be flexible enough to counter the threat. In extreme cases, such as a foreign invasion, the defense must be powerful and immediate.

In most cases, threats are low-level political bribery and graft. The government's regulatory and judiciary agencies are supposed to act like the immune system, identifying crimes, fraud and collusion much like the body's system identifies and eliminates harmful bacteria and viruses. The government's "immune system" is supposed to work in all three elements of the society: community, the marketplace and the government itself.

The Founding Fathers purposefully separated church and state to eliminate religious tyranny, and they granted the State power over commerce to eliminate commercial fraud, predatory lending and the financial exploitation by monopolies and cartels. The free press and governmental oversight agencies were intended to make government transparent and accountable to the citizenry, as fraud, bribery and collusion are difficult in the light of day and under the gaze of impartial regulators.

What the Founding Fathers could not have envisioned is the immense concentration of wealth and political power that has been consolidated in the modern corporation and bank. Though private wealth has always influenced government policy—most of the Founding Fathers were wealthy members of the established Elite—this natural relationship has been transformed as the modern corporation and bank has concentrated unprecedented wealth into new financial Elites.

If the government were still small, this financial power would not be able to buy much political power. But since the State has gained control of the entire economy since World War II, private wealth can now buy immense political power which it uses to eliminate competition and gain privileges.

The amount of money controlled by these new financial Elites is almost beyond conception. For example, a few years ago the average earnings of top hedge fund managers were $600 million. That is not a typo: $600 million each. That is equivalent to the gross domestic product (GDP) of small countries or the entire budget of a major American city government.

Bank-owned assets are $14 trillion, 130% of the entire private-sector gross domestic product (GDP).

For those employed in government agencies, this scale of wealth offers powerful incentives. To name but one example of many, a former government official can command $100,000 per lecture now that he works for a lobbying firm. That is two years of household income earned in one hour. Who pays him $100,000 for an hour-long talk? Those who seek access to government policy makers, that's who.

Every politician who is not independently wealthy needs to raise millions of dollars to fund a costly media-based election campaign. A private lunch with the incumbent might cost $100,000 per person.

To an individual, earning $100,000 for an hour's remarks is a tremendous sum of money. To a politician seeking campaign contributions, $100,000 is serious money. To a fund manager earning $600 million a year or a bank that controls $1 trillion in assets, that $100,000 is small change.

This is how immense private wealth influences government policy and regulations.

The Founding Fathers expected the Supreme Court to weed out power grabs and exploitation, but unfortunately the Supreme Court has failed to do so. In granting corporations the rights of individual citizens, the court has given corporations a free hand to buy political influence and control of the media. By allowing a private consortium of private banks (the Federal Reserve) to act as the central bank of the U.S., the court has allowed banks to control the nation's financial system.

The big banks have used government policies to expand to the point that they now hold the government and nation hostage: they are now "too big to fail," meaning that the government has to bail them out lest they bring down the country's financial system.

What many people forget is that it was government policy that enabled the banks to swallow competitors and become "too big to fail." Without government intervention, these banks would have failed a long time ago when they were much smaller and less dangerous.

If the government and Federal Reserve did not have so much power, they would not have been able to grant the banks so many privileges, nor would they have had the power to bail out private corporations with taxpayer money.

According to the Government Accounting Office (GAO) audit of the Federal Reserve, $16 trillion was handed to the banks in the financial crisis. That's larger than the entire GDP of the U.S.A. ($15 trillion) and much larger than all residential mortgages in America ($10 trillion).

The Founding Fathers envisioned a small, protective government. What we have now is a massive, sprawling government that controls every aspect of the economy and society "from the top down."

The Founding Fathers envisioned a government of checks and balances, a system that could identify internal threats and fix itself much like our body's immune system repairs damage and eliminates harmful bacteria. Sadly, concentrations of wealth and power have crippled our government's immune system; it can no longer fix itself. The Status Quo is now dependent on corruption, fraud, hiding the truth and promises that cannot be met. The leadership has been compromised by their involvement in perpetuating the system; it's as if our government has an auto-immune disease and is destroying itself.

The Central State's controls have been set on "run to fail," i.e. continue on the present course until the machine breaks down.

Any organism or system that lacks a functioning immune system—the ability to repair itself—will expire once it catches a common cold. It is extremely susceptible to any instability, however minor.

The Government and Central Planning

It has been lost to living memory, but not so long ago the average person rarely felt the presence of the Central Government (what political scientists call "the State") in everyday life. The State was limited to a small professional military, Federal courts and an excise tax that touched few citizens directly. Life did not revolve around Federal government regulations or payments.

The memory of a stock market and economy that aren't centrally managed has also been lost. The Federal Reserve constantly intervenes in the markets to manage our perception of the economy's health, and it benefits the politically powerful banking cartel by buying trillions of dollars of questionable assets.

Life without cash payments from the State (called "transfer payments" because the government transfers cash to individuals) is now difficult to recall or even imagine: of the nation's 307 million residents, 47 million residents obtain Food Stamps (SNAP) from the State and 57 million draw Social Security benefits. Medicare pays all but a fraction of the healthcare expenses of 47 million, millions more work directly for the government or serve in the Armed Forces, and regulatory agencies control or influence virtually every aspect of everyday life and enterprise.

These examples merely scratch the surface of State control. Where citizens once had little if any contact with the central government, now the majority of citizens either draw a direct payment from the State or are beholden to the State, which has concentrated what were once widely distributed activities and investments into enormous bureaucracies.

This concentration of power offers irresistible opportunities for those seeking to turn that power to their private advantage. Private concentrations of wealth now have tremendous incentives to influence the State to further their own interests.

For every legitimate control (monitoring and enforcing water quality, for example) performed by the State, there are others that enable private gain behind the auspices of public protection: the agencies tasked with preventing predatory lending, for example, stood by as banks and mortgage lenders committed widespread fraud during the housing bubble. Since the banks control the regulatory machinery with campaign contributions and lobbying, virtually no one was prosecuted for fraud.

This highlights the contradiction at the very core of the Federal government: to protect our freedoms of speech, faith, movement, enterprise and association, the citizens grant the Central State unique power. The central government alone has the power to regulate, tax, induct into the Armed Forces, interrogate citizens and prosecute Federal crimes. But that power is turned to serve private self-interest by concentrations of wealth, and the State's own feeble "immune system" has proven incapable of thwarting this influence.

Government Buys Our Support with Promises That Can't Be Kept

Back when the Federal government was small, it did not pass out payments to millions of citizens. Elections centered on policies, not "transfer payments" to individuals. Education was left to the states and counties.

Now that the Federal government issues payments to roughly half of all households, the incentives have changed. Now people want to protect their payments, and the more the government promises in cash and entitlements, the more people will support the Status Quo, even if it is destroying the country.

Their interests as citizens have been replaced by self-interest in getting cash and entitlements.

This has distorted the citizen-government relationship.

We need to understand just how impossible the government promises have become.

Let's take Medicare as an example. Medicare is paid by a 2.9% payroll tax paid by employees and employers. The median wage for a fulltime worker in the U.S. is about $40,000. Over a thirty year work career, the worker will have earned about $1.2 million, and he and his employer will have paid about $35,000 in total Medicare taxes.

Medicare typically pays between $393,000 and $525,000 in medical costs per person from the time they qualify for coverage (age 65) and the end of their lives. This is roughly ten times the total lifetime taxes paid into the system by fulltime workers.

Basic math and common sense tell us that the system needs 10 workers for every beneficiary to be sustainable. But there are only three workers for every beneficiary now, and only two of those workers have fulltime jobs. Of the roughly 150 million people filing income tax returns in the U.S., 38 million earn less than $10,000 annually. Their contributions to Medicare are minimal; over a lifetime of work, these workers' Medicare contributions will total $1,000 or less.

So there are only two full-time wage earners now for every Medicare beneficiary.

Does anyone seriously think that we can each pay in $35,000 and take out $350,000?

The psychology of dependence and entitlement leads us to ignore reality and focus on what we "deserve." This is one reason why the entitlement mentality is so destructive to individuals and the nation.

In corrupt democracies such as India, politicians openly buy votes with cash. In the U.S., politicians also buy votes, but they do so with entitlements paid by the taxpayer.

The Tyranny of the Majority

Some of the Founding Fathers were worried about the possibility of "the tyranny of the majority," where a majority could impose tyranny on a minority via the ballot box. For example, a religious majority could oppress members of a minority religion by "legally" electing representatives of the majority who passed "legal" laws oppressing the minority.

The Founding Fathers thought that the Bill of Rights and the Supreme Court would protect the citizenry from the tyranny of the majority, but they did not foresee income taxes and entitlements. Roughly half of American wage earners pay little or no Federal income tax. They pay the employees' shares of the Social Security and Medicare payroll taxes (7.65%), but they pay no income tax. The top 10% of households earn 43% of all income and pay 70% of the tax, while the top 25% pay 87% of the income taxes. The lower 50% of households earn 13% of all income and pay 2% of the taxes.

It is well-known that the super-wealthy, the top 1/10th of 1%, have lobbyists and tax attorneys to arrange tax loopholes and exemptions that lower their effective tax rate to 17% of their total income. The high-wage earners pay about double that rate. If we add in property taxes, and state and local taxes, many self-employed middle-class taxpayers are paying 50% or more in taxes.

For example, the self-employment tax is 15.3%, the basic Federal tax rate is 25%, and the typical state income tax rate is around 5%. That adds up to 45%. Now add in property taxes, which are over $10,000 per year in many areas, and the self-employed homeowner taxpayer might be paying over 50% of their income in taxes, not even counting sales taxes.

The Founding Fathers could not have anticipated an America where the government collects 50% of a household's income in taxes, or an America where citizens pay $1 of tax (for example, in Medicare tax) and expect to take out $10. The Founding Fathers could not have anticipated an American government borrowing 35% to 40% of its expenses, each and every year, basically living off a giant credit card. They could not foresee a Federal budget where two-thirds of the money is "direct transfers" to individuals.

Many people claim that we could "balance the budget" if we eliminated foreign aid, cut government waste, trimmed the defense budget, got rid of welfare cheats, taxed the rich more, and so on. Unfortunately, this is wishful thinking; none of these measures would balance the budget. Foreign aid is less than 1% of the budget; defense spending is about 30%, so a 10% cut would only trim the Federal budget by 3%, and so on down the list. Not one of these cuts yields more than a few percent.

As for taxing the rich: the top 1% pays about 37% of all Federal income taxes. (The top 10% pay 70% of all Federal taxes.) Let's assume the top 1% should pay 50% more than what they're currently paying. (Their average tax rate of 24% is less than the 35% rate paid by upper-middle class wage earners.)

I personally believe that it is both fair and necessary that all wealthy taxpayers pay the same rate as self-employed people, which is 15.3% self-employment tax and 25% Federal income tax for a total of 40.3%. But to keep things simple, let's figure a 50% increase in what they pay now.

Increasing the tax rate the wealthy pay would raise an additional $200 billion, as individual income taxes total about $1.1 trillion.

This extra tax revenue would lower the Federal deficit to $1.1 trillion from $1.3 trillion—not enough to change the negative outcome of trillion-dollar deficits as far as the eye can see. But Federal spending won't stay at its current level; it will go up dramatically as the 75 million citizens in the Baby Boom are starting to claim their Social Security and Medicare benefits.

How about taxing corporations? Corporations are not citizens, and in general their loyalty is to their shareholders. To compete in a global economy, they move production facilities and offices around the world, to be close to their major markets and to reap favorable tax rates. Corporations that pay much higher taxes than their competitors are at a competitive disadvantage, and so corporations naturally seek to minimize their tax burden. Governments often offer low tax rates to encourage corporations to expand in their nation.

Experts generally agree that we would collect more taxes from corporations doing business in the U.S. if we lowered the tax rate and eliminated the thousands of pages of tax code that give special treatment to companies that have bought political influence.

If corporation taxes doubled, that would lower the deficit by around $150 - $200 billion. Taxing the rich and doubling corporate taxes would reduce the deficit to about $1 trillion, but not for long, as 10,000 Baby Boomers a day start collecting benefits from Social Security and Medicare. Every year from now until 2029, about four million more Boomers will start collecting Social Security and Medicare. Estimates of the shortfall between what has been promised and what can be collected in taxes start at $134 trillion and run higher, depending on the assumptions of economic growth.

What we don't want to admit is that an economy that is stagnant, an economy where 95% of the workers are earning less year after year, cannot pay benefits that are rising year after year.

What Americans do not want to understand is that two-thirds of the Federal budget is Medicare, Medicaid, Social Security and other direct transfers. One-third of every check from the Federal government is borrowed from our children and grandchildren, who are not represented because they cannot vote.

We already live in a Tyranny of the Majority. Adult recipients of entitlements are borrowing trillions of dollars from a minority who is without a political voice, our children and grandchildren.

The majority of taxpayers pay very little Federal income tax (every employee pays payroll taxes to fund Medicare and Social Security, but these are not income taxes). A minority (25%) pays almost 90% of all the income taxes. This minority is already living in a Tyranny of the Majority, for the majority supports programs that are paid for by the minority who pay most of the taxes. The minority who pays most of the taxes will be outvoted by the majority collecting most of the entitlements.

What is the minority's only choice to escape the tyranny of high taxes? Stop making so much money: retire, sell their business, or simply work less. As the number of high earners declines, the government will collect less tax, and so it will either raise taxes on the remaining high earners or borrow more. Both paths lead to collapse. Remember the household that borrows 40% of its expenses?

Nobody wants to admit any of this. As noted earlier, when the system breaks down, everybody has an excuse; as Voltaire said, no snowflake in an avalanche ever feels responsible. But we are responsible. The only question is whether we accept our responsibility or run from it.

The Psychology of Dependence

When a government's leaders promise entitlements to everyone, regardless of the nation's ability to pay the costs, it is basically a bribe to gain the political support of the recipients. This bribe works as long as the system can support the promised benefits. But as the ratio of workers to retirees and dependents drops, the promises made exceed the available surplus, and the system goes broke.

Remember the key concept: we can only spend surplus, or borrow against future surplus.

Right now the Federal government is borrowing over $1.3 trillion a year—over one-third of the entire budget. Direct payments are about two-thirds of all government spending, so we are borrowing against future surpluses to fund entitlements in the present. Eventually, all tax revenue will be committed to paying interest on the trillions of dollars we've borrowed to pay entitlements. There will be nothing left to invest in the economy or fund other government responsibilities.

This arrangement is clearly unsustainable, and every serious person who examines the facts reaches this self-evident conclusion. But the psychology of dependence has so distorted our thinking that we no longer accept reality.

Dependence takes many forms. Children and teens living at home are dependent on their parents and welfare recipients and "corporate welfare" beneficiaries are dependent on the government.

On the surface, it may seem that dependents should be happy because someone else supplies their needs and they are free of the burden of competing. But dependence has a hidden cost: the dependent has no autonomy, and their dependence saps their self-worth. Self-worth is based on autonomy, self-reliance and a productive role in society. The dependent has none of these sources of self-worth, and so he falls into resentment and an aggrieved focus on perceived injustices. Dependents obsess over what others are getting and resent those in the "parent" role.

Teens chafe at their lack of independence but are as yet unprepared for productive roles in society. Cash payments place the recipient in the role of the teen: it's easier to take the free money than it is to make a go of it on your own, but the cost in self-worth and self-reliance is higher than we imagine.

Eventually, the dependent has lost so much self-confidence that they are terrified of losing the "free money." They have lost the ability to get through life without it, even as they resent their dependence and wish they could be independent.

Political bribery in the form of cash payments leads to a society of resentful, self-absorbed, unproductive dependents. Many face the future with little self-confidence because dependence has eroded their ability to accept risk, make realistic assessments and persevere in the face of setbacks.

There is one other negative consequence of dependence on the Central State. When an individual receives cash from the government, he no longer needs other people's help or attention. He doesn't need his family, friends, neighbors or colleagues: all his needs are now filled by the government. He withdraws into a distorted world without reciprocity; he is free to indulge in frivolous pastimes and has no need to concern himself with the needs of others. The most important relationship in his life is his tie to the government because that's the source of his money.

In place of meaningful contributions to others, he shares resentments with other dependents and whiles away his time unproductively. The government check has isolated him from the community because he no longer needs to contribute to the community to earn his keep. He is alienated from the productive world and cut off from positive sources of self-worth and meaning.

In this way, government transfers destroy community. "Free money" destroys self-reliance and self-confidence, and dependence erodes the ability to be productive in the real world—the foundation of self-worth and meaningful life.

Central Planning Doesn't Work in Complex Systems

One of the pivotal changes in American society over the past 60 years is the rise of the idea that the Federal Government and the Federal Reserve should manage the economy so there will never be another recession or decline in the stock market.

This is unrealistic, as business follows a cycle of credit expansion and contraction. Recessions and stock market declines are healthy; they're like getting a fever to fight an infection. Credit that was extended to projects and people that default must be written off, and stock markets that rise into speculative bubbles must be allowed to "re-set" to reality.

Otherwise, the economy and the stock market is like a person who is never allowed to catch a cold; when they finally get sick, their immune system is so weak that they perish.

Natural systems like the weather are not constant; they swing back and forth between extremes, as all the parts of the system seek equilibrium. The government's goal of manipulating the economy so it grows constantly is like trying to make it rain every day at the same time: that's not how systems work. Rainfall swings back and forth between drought and flooding, while generally remaining between these extremes.

Natural systems do not need governmental intervention to function properly. All the different moving parts contribute their influences, and the system adjusts as a result of millions of inputs.

The government tries to control our complex economy and society by manipulating specific inputs. Can any human know more than the system itself?

A complex system seeks dynamic equilibrium as millions of moving parts and decisions interact in millions of transactions. Fluctuations—what systems analysts call low-level instability—is present throughout the system.

Central planning tries to force the system to respond in a desired way by suppressing natural ebb and flow fluctuations with brute-force interventions. Central planning is the hallmark of totalitarian and Communist regimes, and the failure of these regimes is evidence that manipulation never works for long.

Central Planning and Monoculture

Central Planning is like bulldozing 500 small farms and orchards and planting only soy beans on the cleared land. This is called monoculture. Where pests and diseases could not knock out all the diverse crops and trees on 500 farms, the one-crop monoculture is extremely vulnerable to any pest or disease that finds a single vulnerability in its immune system.

In a diverse financial system, 500 banks would offer loans and pay interest at whatever rates made competitive sense to their management. The Federal Reserve has bulldozed all diversity in the banking system, as it alone sets the interest rate. As a result of this central planning, dozens of banks have been consolidated into five "too big to fail" banks.

Diversity and competition create resilience. Take away diversity and competition and you create vulnerability. Sure enough, this reduction in financial diversity caused the financial system to collapse in 2008.

If the Federal government and the Federal Reserve were actually good at central planning, then why did the dot-com stock market bubble arise and pop, wiping out trillions of dollars in wealth? Why did the housing bubble arise and pop, wiping out trillions of dollars in real wealth? Why did the financial system melt down in 2008, wiping out trillions of dollars in wealth?

It's not just that the few individuals at the top of these institutions are incompetent—no central planning agency can replace the intelligence of complex, transparent systems. All central planning is incompetent by its very nature.

Central Planning Increases the Risk of Collapse

In our economy, the Central State and Federal Reserve have taken control of the money supply, the interest rate, the qualifications for home mortgages (FHA loans), the guarantees to mortgage lenders, and the statistical measures of the economy.

The irony is that the more the State tries to control, the more power it has to disrupt the system.

The government tries to limit the risk of "bad things happening" by taking more and more control of the economy, but the more control it takes, the greater the risk that its interventions will disrupt the system.

This is the unintended consequence of trying to control complex systems by manipulating a few levers. The more you intervene in a heavy-handed fashion, the higher the risk that you will disrupt the entire system.

The Central State and bank try to overcome this flaw by taking control of even more levers. They think that by controlling everything, they can lower risk, but they're only increasing risk, because a handful of levers can never control a complex system with millions of inputs.

For example of this, let's look at how the Federal Reserve (America's privately owned central bank) tries to manage the economy by pulling two levers: money supply and the interest rate.

The Federal Reserve's Grand Failure to Manage the Economy

The Federal Reserve is presumed to have almost supernatural powers to fix whatever ails the economy. But the Fed only has two levers to pull:

1. The Fed can manipulate interest rates to near-zero
2. The Fed can print and shove "free money" to the banks

That's it. Those are all the tools the Fed has in its toolbox. Let's consider what these tools accomplish in the real world.

Zero interest rates do not cause potential employers to hire unemployed people. Zero interest rates incentivize financial speculation (yield-chasing via trading risk assets) and malinvestment in marginal projects that would be left on the drawing board if rates were not super-low.

Low interest rates also lead to money flowing to marginal borrowers. If rates were 10%, only those with good credit, credible income and ample collateral qualify for loans. At 1%, marginal borrowers (the kind who are most likely to default) qualify for loans.

All the Fed accomplishes with zero-interest rates is to build up a new wave of borrowers who will default. The Fed's policy of encouraging more debt and leverage simply adds to the mountain of impaired debt that is crushing the economy.

The Fed's zero-interest rate policy (ZIRP) has effectively stolen hundreds of billions of dollars in interest from savers and pension funds. Recent calculations are that savers and pension funds lost $1.5 trillion in interest since 2009, thanks to the Fed's zero-interest rate policy. The unintended consequences are disastrous: the Fed's ZIRP punishes the prudent and rewards financier gamblers.

Pushing "free money" to the banks was supposed to do three things: It was supposed to enable the banks to lend money at a premium that generated enormous profits that could be used to rebuild their balance sheets.

Here's how this works: the Fed lends banks money at 0%, and the banks make student loans at 7%. The banks get to keep the 7% as pure profit.

The banks can't default on their loans from the Fed, because there's no interest due. It is truly 'free money." The students aren't so lucky: if they default, they are hounded and harassed for the rest of their lives, as student loans cannot be erased in bankruptcy.

This is what happens in a centrally planned economy: corruption, injustice, favoritism for the super-wealthy.

The Fed's zero-interest rate policy (ZIRP) was supposed to spur consumption and investment, because money was so "cheap" that consumers and businesses would both be encouraged to borrow more. But what it actually did was encourage malinvestment and speculation, the exact opposite of productive investment.

Lastly, it was supposed to enable homeowners to refinance their underwater mortgages at lower rates, creating more disposable income that the homeowners would then spend on more consumption.

But you can't force people to borrow money, and offering marginal borrowers more debt does not make them creditworthy. The truth is that 95% of American households have taken on ever-rising debt loads while their inflation-adjusted incomes have remained flat-lined.

The Fed's "solution" to over-indebtedness and excessive leverage is to encourage more debt and more leverage. But the lower 95% of households don't qualify for new loans or refinancing because they already have too much debt, and risk-averse banks have tightened lending standards.

So the Fed's "free money" is dead money. It isn't funding new enterprises; it's sitting in banks as reserves or funding speculative bets in the foreign exchange, stock and bond markets.

Maybe banks added a few traders to play with the Fed's "free money," but that's like hitting the unemployment nail with a handsaw blade: it doesn't do anything in the real economy or the labor market.

Fed Chairman Ben Bernanke's famous "helicopter" from which he drops money into the economy is a misnomer. He can't drop money into the real economy; all he can do is drop it into the banks, where it languishes as reserves or is used to fuel speculative gambles in global markets.

The all-powerful Fed is actually powerless to do anything useful in the real economy. It can fuel speculative stock market rallies, but it can't lower unemployment or erase debts. All it can do is rob savers and pension funds of hundreds of billions of dollars each and every year.

The Fed's Policies Lower Household Income

As I hope you understand by now, the U.S. economy is based on ever-expanding credit: more lending and more borrowing year after year. The Federal Reserve prints money, loans it to the banks at 0% (i.e. "free") and the banks then loan the money to businesses and consumers. The banks profit and the economy grows as people buy more goods and services.

The problem with this model is that household income doesn't rise just because banks have plenty of free money to lend. As we saw in our example of the household that borrows 40% of its budget every year, eventually most of the budget goes to paying interest on the rising debt. Consumption drops because the discretionary income left after paying essential bills and debt drops to zero.

Rising debt leads to a decline in consumption and recession. There is no way to escape this consequence of ever-higher debt.

There is another reason incomes are declining for 95% of American households: inflation. "Free money" from the Fed ends up in commodities such as oil, driving up the price of energy. As the cost of essentials rise while income remains stagnant, households have less income to spend.

A key concept here is "purchasing power." Economists use purchasing power to measure income because nominal income doesn't reflect the reality of how much your money can buy.

Back in the 1970s when the average wage was $7 an hour, $1 bought 20 loaves of bread because a loaf of bread cost 35 cents. Now the average wage is $23 an hour, but the $23 only buys 10 loaves of bread because bread is $2.30 a loaf. The purchasing power of each dollar has fallen in half, even as the nominal wage has more than tripled.

If we adjust for inflation, household incomes have fallen 9% since 2007. Measured in purchasing power, the decline is even steeper.

The more money the Fed prints and loans to the banks, the less our money buys in the real world. So the Fed's policies actually take money away from average American households in three ways:

1. By pushing debt as the way to fund more consumption, more household income goes to pay interest and debts, leaving less for the household to spend, save or invest.

2. Inflation and a loss of purchasing power means every dollar buys less than it did in the past.

3. The Fed's zero-interest rate policy (ZIRP) means households earn virtually nothing on their savings, retirement accounts and money market funds, so their non-earned income has plummeted to near zero. Adjusted for inflation, we're losing money on savings, money market funds and short-term bonds.

The Failure of the Fed's "Wealth Effect"

The Federal Reserve has a plan to get around the decline in household income, and it's based on the "wealth effect." The wealth effect simply means that when the assets you own go up in value, you feel wealthier and are more prone to borrow and spend—even if you don't have even one dollar of additional income.

The wealth effect is an *internal psychological state*: it is entirely in the mind, a feeling rather than a fact. If your income rises $100, that is a fact. If the value of your home goes up $1,000, that may give you a feeling of being wealthier but you can't actually get your hands on that $1,000 unless you sell your home.

The Federal Reserve creates the wealth effect by inflating assets in speculative bubbles. As we have seen in our casino example, free money at 0% interest rates leads to speculators gambling wildly with other people's money because they have nothing to lose and much to gain.

Fed chairman Ben Bernanke has explicitly stated this is the goal of Fed policy: "If people feel that their financial situation is better because their 401k (retirement account) looks better for whatever reason, or their house is worth more, they are more willing to go out and provide the demand (i.e. buy things)."

There are two problems with blowing speculative investment bubbles to jack up asset values to spark the wealth effect. One is that speculative bubbles always burst, for the reasons explained in our casino example. The second is that if household income is stagnant, the wealth effect requires borrowing more money, which means more of the household income goes to servicing debt.

There is a third problem with a policy of boosting the wealth effect with speculative bubbles: most American households don't own enough assets to feel much wealthier if assets bubble up in value.

For example, 91% of all stocks (what financial professionals call "equities") are owned by the top 20% of households. The top 10% own 81%, and the top 1% own almost 40%. Stock ownership is highly concentrated in the very households that have high incomes and don't need to borrow to consume. While the debt loads of 95% of American households have kept rising for decades, the top 5% have paid down their household debt.

The top 5% don't need to feel wealthier—they are wealthier. The Fed's "Jedi mind trick"—the wealth effect—only works on the 95% who are actually poorer and more heavily in debt every year.

Unfortunately, the Fed's plan has one last devastating consequence: once a speculative bubble starts rising, people naturally join the crowd and pour their hard-earned money into the asset that's bubbling higher.

Then, when the bubble bursts, they lose their hard-earned money. This is what happened in the dot-com stock market and the housing bubble. Over 30% of homeowners with mortgages are now "underwater" as house values have declined: their mortgage is higher than the value of their home. About 30% of homeowners have no mortgage, and have no interest in going into debt; they are immune to the wealth effect.

Millions of other homeowners still have some equity in their homes but are no longer creditworthy enough to borrow more: their high levels of debt and stagnant incomes makes them a poor risk for more loans.

For all these reasons, the Federal Reserve's attempts to spark the wealth effect have not just failed—they've destroyed trillions of dollars in income and wealth. They have had catastrophically negative consequences.

Understanding the Expansion of Government

We take it for granted that the government (Federal, state and local) dominates our society and economy, but this was not always the case. In the early 19th century, government was modest in size.

The main reason for this was the nation's surplus was not large enough to support a big government. Remember that we can only spend as much as we generate in surplus. Back in the early 1800s, most Americans lived and worked on farms that did not generate much surplus. The government couldn't be very big because people didn't have much surplus to pay in taxes.

One way to understand surplus and the size of government is to consider a subsistence farming community where each family and village only ekes out enough to feed themselves and set aside seed for the next planting. There is no government because there is no surplus to pay for government.

Government is a luxury that is only possible if people create enough surpluses to pay for it.

Something miraculous happened in 1859 in Pennsylvania: oil was found, and the U.S. was to become the Saudi Arabia of the early 20th century. Our vast oil resources were cheap to tap, and this natural resource created gigantic surpluses.

In my book *Resistance, Revolution, Liberation: A Model for Positive Change* I identified five types of capitalism. Extractive Capitalism is based on the surplus reaped by the extraction of an easy-to-get natural resource. This resource is like "found money" because at first it is easy to extract and generates huge surpluses. Once the easy-to-get resource is depleted, the cost of extraction goes up and the surpluses drop.

Take the discovery of gold in California in 1849 as an example. Once the easy-to-get gold was extracted, the boom collapsed, leaving ghost towns behind.

Now that the U.S. has burned through its cheap-to- extract oil, the surpluses generated by energy extraction have declined. Yes, there are vast quantities of unconventional oil and offshore oil, but these are not cheap to extract. Even if there is a nearly unlimited supply of these unconventional oils, they cost so much to extract and process that the surplus is much less than in the good old days.

This is the meaning of EROIE—"energy returned on energy invested." In the good old days, the energy in one barrel of oil extracted and refined 100 barrels of oil. Today, it takes the energy of one barrel of oil to extract and refine three barrels of unconventional oil. The point is that it's not just abundance that sets the cost and surplus, it's the cost of production.

The industrial revolution harnessed this cheap energy to dramatically boost productivity of labor with machines and assembly lines. The communication revolution led by telegraph, radio, television and the Internet has further increased productivity. The second industrial revolution led by computers, software and robotics has unleashed a new wave of productivity gains.

These improvements flow from enterprise capitalism, the entrepreneurial model we associate with companies such as Apple. In this form of capitalism, an open market allows new enterprises to start from scratch, and then rewards capital invested early in the enterprise. It heaps the greatest gains on innovations that improve productivity.

The success of this model created large surpluses that enabled America and Europe to vastly expand their governments. In countries such as France, the Central State absorbs 50% of the nation's GDP. In the U.S. government absorbs about one-third of our GDP.

For a number of reasons we will cover later, surplus in advanced economies are declining. Yet governments aren't declining, they're continuing to expand year after year. To fill the widening gap between the surplus available to spend on government and the government's ever-expanding budget, the government borrows money every year. This is the deficit. In the U.S., it's about $1.3 trillion a year, over one-third of all government spending, and almost 10% of the nation's total output (GDP).

From our household example, we know what happens to governments that borrow 40% of their spending every year: they collapse under the weight of the accumulated debt and interest. Remember that debt has another destructive trait: it drains the pool of money that's available to invest in the future. Once this pool has been drained, increases in productivity decline and the household, business or nation becomes poorer, and less able to generate future surpluses and investment.

If you consume your seed corn, you have nothing to plant next year. Borrowing endless trillions of dollars that accrue interest is like eating our nation's seed corn. It sets up what is known as diminishing returns. Diminishing returns is like running on a treadmill that's constantly speeding up: you have to run faster just to stay in the same place.

Ever-expanding debt is like a treadmill that speeds up: more and more of your surpluses go to paying interest, and there is less and less to invest in future productivity.

The more debt you have, the more interest and principal you have to pay, and the less surplus you have to spend on luxuries such as government.

We refuse to recognize that our national surplus is no longer large enough to support our gigantic government because we don't want to lose the cash "direct transfers" we're receiving or that we've been promised. Remember, those direct transfers to individuals are two-thirds of the budget; trimming around the edges won't fix anything.

We can only spend what we generate in surplus, and if we spend all of that on government, there is not enough left to invest in future productivity. The more we borrow to enable government spending, the more we pay in interest. The less we invest in the future, the less surplus we'll have to spend in the future.

Debt goes up, investment goes down, and we're trapped in a cycle of diminishing returns that eventually leads to collapse. This is the result of letting our government become larger than our surplus.

How Governments Become Inefficient and Corrupt

There are four conditions in a healthy government and economy:
1. Transparency
2. Competition
3. Accountability
4. Risk is recognized

Transparency and competition and two sides of the same coin: without transparency, competition cannot exist. If the government allows "backroom deals" known only to a few, transparency is lost. Those are the outside have lost the advantage to those few "in the know."

If the government passes an obscure tax law designed to benefit one company, the company's competitors lose ground not through their own doing but by State intervention on behalf of their competitor.

Accountability is the connection of action with consequence: failure and inefficiency must be corrected, or the system ends up draining surplus from the successful and efficient to subsidize the failed and inefficient.

Risk is ever-present in life and cannot be eliminated; it can only be shared or transferred.

Whenever risk appears to have vanished, it has only been shared or transferred to others. You cannot eliminate risk, any more than you can eliminate gravity.

When the government intervenes in the economy or guarantees someone or a company against any loss, it is absorbing the risk of failure. If the government guarantees enough people and companies against loss, the risks of failure are piled up into a mountain so large that the government itself is at risk of failure.

Remember, risk cannot be eliminated; it can only be shared or transferred.

To understand how the State (the central government) becomes corrupt and cripples the economy, we first need to understand how capitalism works. There are four essential conditions for a capitalist economy:

1. Capital (cash) is placed at risk (invested) for an uncertain gain (profit).
2. Capital fluidly seeks the highest available profit.
3. Transparent markets discover the price of goods, services, equities, debt and risk.
4. Innovation offers competitive advantages in transparent (open, free) markets.

These are the keys of classical capitalism.

But we cannot truly understand capitalism unless we see its unwholesome underbelly, which are the great profits that can be reaped by eliminating competition and transparency.

For example, in the early 20th century, John D. Rockefeller bought up or forced out all his competitors in the oil industry and established a monopoly that allowed him to make bigger profits than were otherwise possible. If you can establish a monopoly, you can charge whatever you want, because there are no competitors to offer a lower price or better service.

So the single best way to dramatically lower risk and increase profit is to eradicate competition and create a monopoly or a cartel that controls the supply and price.

The next best way to lower risk and increase gain is to eliminate transparency so price can be manipulated to your advantage.

The biggest monopoly is the government itself. It holds a monopoly on lawmaking, the justice system, the military and the nation's money.

Once the government has its hands in every aspect of the economy, the easiest way to eliminate competition is to have the government do it for you.

Once special privileges have been granted by the State, a cartel is no longer accountable to its customers; it is only accountable to those who create and enforce its special privileges: legislators and regulators.

Here is the critical point: it is only possible for the government to grant special privileges if it controls and regulates the entire economy. If its role is limited, so are its powers to grant special privileges.

This expansion of government power feeds corruption, because it becomes "cheaper" for companies to influence legislators and regulators than it is to establish competitive advantages in the open market.

For example, it might cost $100 million to develop and market a new product, which might fail and lose money. But a mere $5 million in campaign contributions is enough to "buy" legislation that grants special privileges that erect barriers to competition or reap tax windfalls.

This leverage is only possible if the State has grabbed vast power over the economy. If someone lobbied a legislator in 1830, there was very little that legislator could grant because the government was small. Now that the government dominates the economy and society, the favors that can be granted are equally large.

Put yourself in the shoes of corporate leaders. Why risk $100 million when a $5 million bribe to key legislators will generate guaranteed profits with no risk? It makes "good business sense" to persuade the government to "regulate" to your advantage.

This is why the tax code is thousands of pages in length and why legislation regulating the financial and healthcare sectors is thousands of pages long: there are hundreds of special privileges that must be granted.

One key feature of all this legislative and regulatory complexity is the lack of transparency. Consider healthcare in the U.S. The cost of hospital care is completely opaque; the final bill is manipulated according to who is paying. The "price" might be $100,000, but Medicare pays only $30,000 and an insurance company pays $50,000. When the price and supply are hidden, consumers are unable to compare price and quality, and so prices are high and quality is low. This is the consequence when transparency is lost.

Whenever the government grants a special privilege or issues a promise or guarantee, accountability is lost. If someone is promised lifetime employment regardless of their productivity, failure and laziness are "rewarded" because there is no consequence to failing or being inefficient.

The efficient subsidize the inefficient. The system's incentives switch from success and efficiency to failure and inefficiency.

The more power the government accumulates, the more bureaucratic opportunities there are to avoid accountability. Once the agency is responsible, the individuals within the agency are no longer accountable. Failed policies continue on untouched because there is no consequence to failure or inefficiency.

When the government becomes gargantuan in size and power, risk is no longer recognized: the government can 'fix" everything with another promise or guarantee.

But risk cannot be eliminated, it can only be transferred. When the government guarantees entitlements, special privileges, tax loopholes, mortgages, pensions and a host of other benefits, the risks of failure and costs of inefficiency haven't vanished; they've simply been transferred to our children and their unborn children.

Governments become corrupt when they take on vast powers. Governments become inefficient when accountability and transparency are lost. When accountability, transparency and competition are lost, efficiency and success subsidize the ever rising costs of failure and inefficiency protected by the government.

When jobs, loopholes, entitlements, pensions, mortgages and privileges are all guaranteed, the risks have been transferred to the government itself. Since inefficiency and corruption have no negative consequence, they are in effect rewarded. As their share of the government and economy increases, the unthinkable happens: the government itself fails, for its promises exceed the surpluses generated by the weakened economy.

The Corrupting Influence of Financialization

One example of this systemic decay of values, rule of law and transparency is the "robo-signing" mortgage scandal in which the major mortgage lenders engaged in practices that flouted the law, not just in processing affidavits but in respecting basic property rights.

In a nation where the rule of law existed in more than name, here's what should have happened:

1. The legal front known as MERS, the mortgage industry's placeholder for mortgage notes, would be summarily shut down.

2. All mortgages, and all derivatives and securities based on mortgages, would be marked-to-market, that is, placed in an open exchange that priced each one in a transparent market.

3. All losses would be declared immediately, and any institution that was deemed insolvent would be shuttered and its assets auctioned off in an orderly fashion.

4. Regardless of the cost to the owners of mortgages, every mortgage, lien and note in the U.S. would be painstakingly traced to the underlying deed and real property, and each document properly filed in each county as per U.S. law.

That none of this has happened is evidence that the rule of law only exists in America when it suits the financial sector that controls the State, the Central Bank and thus the nation. When the rule of law "costs too much" for the financial sector to comply, it is ignored or subverted.

This sacrifice of the rule of law to preserve the financial sector's wealth and power requires the collusion and active participation of the Federal government and the Federal Reserve. The government forgave all the lawlessness in the $10 trillion mortgage industry with a paltry $25 billion settlement, which the banks were supposed to apply to helping homeowners in distress. Instead, the banks are crediting debts that have already been discharged in bankruptcy and "short sales" they had already approved, where the homeowner is allowed to sell the house for less than the mortgage.

In other words, the $25 billion is cost-free to the banks because they are simply crediting losses they had already incurred. The settlement was pure public-relations; it cost the banks nothing to systematically break the nation's laws governing mortgages, documentation and property rights.

The nation's central bank, the Federal Reserve, bought over 10% of all outstanding mortgages in the country, $1.1 trillion worth, with money it created for that purpose, in 2009 and 2010. In September 2012, it announced it would buy an additional $480 billion of mortgages every year, roughly 5% of all outstanding mortgages. Why did the Fed buy 10% of the nation's mortgages? Why is it buying 5% more every year? It did so for two reasons:

1. To remove the impaired mortgages from banks' balance sheets, freeing them from reporting staggering losses, and

2. To bury phantom/illegal mortgages in the Fed's opaque balance sheet.

In the words of analyst Catherine Austin Fitts, "The Fed is now where mortgages go to die." The Federal Reserve is actively laundering phantom and improperly documented mortgages by paying the full value to banks, even though the mortgages are worth a fraction of their full value. All the issues of false documentation in these mortgages disappear from the banks; the mortgages have been "laundered" of legal problems and losses by the Federal Reserve.

Given the magnitude of the Fed's mortgage buying program, this makes the Federal Reserve the largest money-laundering operation in the world, on par with the world's drug cartels.

This is only one example of the erosion of rule of law that is the direct result of financialization and the dominance of the financial sector. The Central State and Central Bank now kowtow to the banks, systematically undermining the nation's values and rule of law to preserve the banking sector's wealth and power.

One of the key mechanisms the State uses to obscure its role in preserving bank power is complexity. When the thicket of regulation becomes impenetrable, I call this a *complexity fortress*. The rules are supposedly transparent, but if they require a staff of 100 experts with advanced degrees to plow through it all, how transparent are they? In practical terms, they are merely part of the shadow systems of finance and governance that have undermined American values, principles and free enterprise.

When the tax code is thousands of pages long and filled with purposefully complex sections written specifically to benefit a handful of corporations, or even a single corporation, how can anyone claim this is a transparent expression of the rule of law?

How much information is actually in 10,000 pages of filings and regulations? The complexity of the information renders it opaque to everyone but those who wrote it. Banks use this illusion of transparency to construct derivatives and securities so complex that the buyers cannot possibly assess the risks involved. This is how towns in Scandinavia came to own mortgage-backed securities that were presented as safe AAA-rated securities by American banks but that were actually highly risky bundles of default-prone, fraudulent mortgages.

When the rules limit bank power, they are either changed or ignored. When the forces that profit from financialization find the nation's transparent systems limit their profits and power, they establish "shadow" systems of banking, finance, offshore tax havens and mortgage securitization that operate outside the light of transparency.

The average American has no idea how deep the shadow systems have reached. So much of modern finance, regulation and governance are safely out of public view in shadow systems or entities that are poorly regulated. Some 90% of the daily activity in the U.S. stock market, for example, is under the control of high-frequency trading computers, and regulators do not even have the proper tools to monitor this activity, even though it is legal.

As noted above, this brazen hijacking of the rule of law by Elites has severely undercut the ethics of non-Elites, many of whom joined in the housing bubble/financialization fraud by lying about their income, debts and the value of the properties they were mortgaging.

What we have now is two systems, one for the political and financial Elites, and one for everyone else. The Elites either ignore the laws that rule the rest of us, or they have their political puppets change the rules as needed. When public outrage wells up, a few underlings are given wrist-slap penalties in a Soviet-style trial designed to show the rule of law still exists. Meanwhile the financial Elites buy protection from the market and from the rule of law.

Here is how 19th-century French economist Frederic Bastiat described this financier-dominated society: *"When plunder becomes a way of life for a group of men in a society, over the course of time they create for themselves a legal system that authorizes it and a moral code that glorifies it.*

But how is this legal plunder to be identified? Quite simply. See if the law takes from some persons what belongs to them, and gives it to other persons to whom it does not belong. See if the law benefits one citizen at the expense of another by doing what the citizen himself cannot do without committing a crime."

If you or I knowingly submitted false affidavits, sold fraudulent mortgages and improperly filed false mortgage documents, the mortgages would be voided and we would be investigated and prosecuted. Yet when "too big to fail" banks systematically do this on a vast scale, no one is investigated or prosecuted, and the Federal Reserve buys and buries the fraudulent mortgages.

America has strayed from the values, principles and qualities that enabled its long rise to widespread prosperity. Those seeking "fixes" by tweaking a policy here or there are fixing nothing. The rot of financialization has weakened all three pillars of prosperity: core values, the intellectual framework and the machinery of governance and free enterprise.

When the State Dominates the Economy, Corruption Is Inevitable

This point is so poorly understood by the general public that it needs to be repeated: when government expands to the point that it dominates the economy, corruption is inevitable. Why?

As described above, private wealth will soon realize that influencing the Central State to grant it special privileges is much cheaper than influencing the open market. (This is also true of private unions, which have also secured special privileges by buying political influence.)

There is another aspect to expanding government power. Once the Central State controls the financial sector, and it allows a rapid expansion of debt and leverage, the sums of money that can be made soar to previously unimagined heights. In the 1950s, finance-related profits accounted for only 5% of American corporate profits. Now they are more than 25% of all corporate profits.

If we recall our examples of leverage, we understand how debt and leverage enable enormous profits from speculative bubbles. These enormous profits give financiers more than enough money to influence government oversight and policy with campaign contributions and lobbying. This lobbying increases their special privileges, so they profit even more, and this cycle feeds an ever-expanding government and financial sector.

Remember that the government benefits greatly from speculative bubbles, too, as tax revenues skyrocket, and those higher tax revenues enable the government to further expand its power. As more and more parts of the economy fall under the control of the Central State, private capital within those industries must influence State policy to protect themselves from more politically powerful competitors.

You see how this works: as the government expands and take more control of the economy, its expansion forces private business (and unions) to influence State regulation and policy to protect themselves from competitors who have already bought privileges from the government.

In this way, the vested interests also expand along with the government, and so does their buying of influence (lobbying and corruption).

As tax revenues swell, the government is pressured to expand its promises, so it promises more welfare, richer pensions, more healthcare, increased defense spending, and so on. But the rising tax revenues are not based on sustainable growth—they're based on speculative bubbles blown by skyrocketing debt and leverage.

Once the government is seen as responsible for propping up every sector of the economy and keeping all the promises it made during boom times, the pressure on the Elites running the government (senior bureaucrats, elected officials, etc.) to "fudge" data becomes irresistible once the economy starts weakening.

This is why the unemployment rate magically declines even as the number of employed stays the same: the "statistical snapshots" that influence our perception of the economy are manipulated to appear positive even when conditions are deteriorating. This is called "managing perceptions," and this explains why the government has entered the "perception management" business. If the public knew that the economy was unsustainable, they might vote out politicians and demand wholesale changes that would limit the privileges of vested interests. Rather than lose power, government Elites "fudge" the data to make the economy look healthy even as it is crumbling.

These Elites are also under tremendous pressure from vested interests (bankers, public unions, etc.) to intervene on their behalf.

In response to these demands, the government lowers interest rates to zero, guarantees lenders against any losses (the casino example above), expand money supply, and so on. As we have seen, all these politically expedient "fixes" only create much bigger problems down the road.

As the unsustainable speculative bubble-boom ends, the government must increase its borrowing to fund all its promises and the guarantees issued to politically powerful vested interests. This establishes another negative self-reinforcing cycle: the government needs to sell bonds to pay for its deficit spending, and it turns to the biggest banks (called "primary dealers") to sell the bonds on the global market. The Central State becomes dependent on the banking sector to sell its bonds (debt), and the banks make money by selling the ever-expanding government debt.

The government's need to sell bonds to fund its rising deficits and the banking sector's need to have debt to sell create an incestuous partnership: the Central State and the financial sector are equally dependent on debt and speculative bubbles, and so each is now dependent on each other.

The incentives to mask the problems created by skyrocketing debt lead both the government and the financial sector to "fudge" the numbers: the State fudges economic statistics, and the financial sector fudges their books. Since they both depend on manipulated numbers to hide the rot in the real economy, they have a strong motivation to fudge numbers and withhold truthful disclosures.

If you fudge the truth, is it the same as lying? Government and financial leaders have convinced themselves that distorting the truth is necessary to keep the Status Quo afloat, and it seems they're right: once a system depends on smoke-and-mirrors accounting, incomplete disclosures, phony projections and all the other tricks of deception, it will collapse once the truth is revealed.

This dependence leads to the "revolving door" between private industry and government. When a top Pentagon official retires, the following week he is offered a plum executive position in a defense contractor.

This is what is called crony capitalism: public and private Elites distribute the nation's wealth to their politically influential cronies. Government funds are squandered on politically expedient "fixes" that serve vested interests, and vast amounts of debt are taken on to pay for unproductive friction.

It is vital that we understand how the expansion of government power inevitably leads to speculative bubbles and financial corruption. As both the government and financial sector have come to depend on ever-expanding debt and leverage for their wealth and power, the interests of the State and finance have aligned.

The shared need to create an illusory view of the economy and to sell gigantic sums of government debt has made the State and the financial sector partners in deception and corruption.

When the data and accounts have been corrupted, reality has been lost. All decisions based on phony numbers will be tragically flawed.

The citizenry grant special powers to the government to protect civil liberties, "the commons" we all share (water, air, national parks, etc.) and minorities against the tyranny of the majority. But in addition to enforcing these essential duties of the State, an over-reaching government that is partnered with vested interests distorts the marketplace and the community to the point that society becomes dysfunctional.

The Employer, the Employee and the Government

Let's say you own a small business with one employee, and the government mandates that you give the employee a 10% raise every year and pay his health insurance, which also goes up by about 10% every year. To protect the worker from any reduction in pay, the government mandates that you pay the worker his full monthly salary even if you cut his hours. To keep unemployment low, the government also mandates that you can't fire an employee except if they are convicted of felony crimes directed against you.

Every enterprise faces risks: key customers could move to competitors or close down, a new competitor could arise with a technological edge you can't match, the global economy could go into recession and hurt your overseas sales, the cost of key components or raw materials could skyrocket, and so on. The risks are constant, variable and unpredictable.

You can buy insurance against theft and fire, sharing those risks with others, and you could buy your raw materials with futures contracts, hedging against the risk of sudden price increases, but you can't eliminate the risks of sales and profit margins declining.

The government rules do not eliminate the risk of business declining; they transfer all the risk to you. In a free market, your employee was also exposed to the risk of business declining. If business fell off, he would face a cut in hours or pay, or even the loss of his job.

By forcing you to increase your employee's pay regardless of the market for your good or service, the government increased the risk of your business going broke: your costs go up every year, even if your sales and profits are plummeting. Since the government prohibits you from laying off your employee, it has transferred all the risk to you. Your employee now has a risk-free job: he cannot be fired or laid off, regardless of business conditions.

Human nature being what it is, your employee responds to this risk-free environment by slacking off. After all, since there's no risk of being fired, why work hard? Why not show up late and take long lunches?

It's like promising every student an A regardless of whether they attend class, do their homework or learn the material. A few might be motivated enough to still work hard, but most students will cut class, stop doing homework and not apply themselves once the class is risk-free. They will do the absolute minimum required to get their promised A.

In the real world, there are consequences to every action. In your business, consequence has vanished for your employee: he can goof off, mess up the work, ignore your instructions, and do whatever he wants short of committing a felony against you, and there are no meaningful consequences for his actions.

Like risk, consequences don't really vanish, either; they are simply transferred to somebody else.

Now all the risks and consequences are on you.

With business deteriorating and your employee slacking off, the losses start mounting. Soon you are borrowing money every month to pay the employee, who now expects his paycheck and benefits rain or shine. In his mind, this is what he deserves and what he's earned. In his mind, thanks to government guarantees, he's not in the hole with you; you're in the hole by yourself.

The financial hole you're in deepens until you've run out of credit and can't borrow any more money to cover your losses. Even though the government mandated that you can't fire your employee, it didn't give you the right to print money to do so.

You have no choice but to close your business. You have been wiped out, partly because business conditions went downhill but also because all the risk and consequence was transferred to you by the government.

The government issues you a stern warning that you face penalties for laying off your employee, but as the saying has it, you can't get blood from a stone. You have no more money to pay your employee or the government penalty. There is nothing left to squeeze out of you.

The government assumed it could mandate reality, but reality is like the tide: the government can order it not to go out, but it will go out anyway, for it is driven by forces beyond the control of the government.

Your employee is in disbelief: you can't fire me, the government said I had a permanent job here. Since risk and consequence cannot be mandated away, it turns out nothing the State mandates is permanent. When the State orders the tide to come in, and it happens to be coming in anyway, then it looks like the tide is following the State's orders.

But when the tide recedes, the State's mandates are revealed as illusory. Nothing is permanent simply because the government ordered it.

Risk and consequence are laws of Nature, and they cannot be repealed. They can only be transferred to somebody else. But when the few saddled with all the risk go down, they act like dominoes, toppling everyone who thought they were living in a risk-free, consequence-free fantasyland.

The government itself is like the employee: regardless of how the economic tides are flowing, it wants its guaranteed income (taxes) from the productive.

The State Cannot Repeal Risk, It Can Only Transfer It

All government entitlements—Social Security, Medicare, Medicaid, pensions and so on—are unlimited promises. There is no limit on what these programs spend on those who qualify; they must spend whatever has been promised to everyone who qualifies. But the economic tide doesn't just come in, it also goes out. When the tide is going out, the economy generates fewer surpluses. In a household or business, the reduction in surplus would lead to reduced spending.

Remember: we can only spend surplus. If we eat our seed corn, we will have nothing to invest in future planting. If we borrow money to make up for the reduced income, we have to pay back with interest, which reduces future surpluses.

Entitlements transfer all the risk of an economic downturn from the recipients to the taxpayers. Since the government can't limit entitlement spending, it either borrows money to pay for the entitlements, passing the higher interest payments onto future generations, or it raises taxes on taxpayers, reducing their income.

Remember, there are only four things we can do with the surplus we generate:

1. consume it
2. waste it on friction
3. invest it in future production
4. pay interest

If we spend the entire surplus on consumption, waste and interest payments, there is none left to invest in the future, and the enterprise—household, business or nation—goes into a downward death spiral of diminishing surplus, investment and productivity.

When the economic tide is receding fast, the government borrows from the future to pay today's entitlements. This puts the risk and consequence on future taxpayers. Since higher interest deprives future generations of money to invest in their future, this is the equivalent of eating our seed corn.

We aren't borrowing from people we don't know; we're borrowing from our children and grandchildren.

Those drawing entitlements have been promised benefits based on the idea that the tide would always be coming in and the economy would be generating more surplus every year. But the tide recedes as often as it rises, and so as surpluses shrink more of what's left is spent on entitlements and interest on rising debt.

This is what's called a positive feedback loop, or a self-reinforcing trend. As investment declines, so does production and surplus. As more of the dwindling surplus is spent on entitlements and other current consumption, there is even less to invest in the future. As investment is starved, productivity declines and surpluses shrink even faster.

Assuming that the tide will only rise and never recede is like assuming we can repeal gravity. By transferring the risk and consequence of economic downturn from the government and entitlement programs to private-sector taxpayers, we've created a situation just like the employer-employee business described above.

The employee is protected from any risk, not because risk was repealed, but because it was transferred to the employer. The risk and consequence pile up on the employer, driving him into bankruptcy. At that point the risk, which was temporarily suppressed by the government intervention, erupts and strikes the employee with full force: he loses his job and his benefits.

The government cannot repeal risk and consequence; it can only transfer them to others. When those few buckle under the pressures, the entire system crumbles.

Transferring risk and consequence always backfires. You can share risk, but you can't transfer it to someone else. Eventually it takes down the people you transferred it to, and then it takes everyone else down, even those who believed they were living in a risk-free wonderland.

The government can claim that it has repealed risk and consequence, and that 307 million people will get what was promised to them regardless of the economic tides, but this is a false promise. All we're doing is borrowing money from our children and grandchildren and spending it on ourselves. We're eating the nation's seed corn, whether we have the courage to admit it or not.

The tides can't be ordered around by the government, and we can't argue our way out of a hole.

The State and Opportunity Cost

In an open market economy, risk and consequence are spread evenly amongst all participants, buyers and sellers alike. In a government-run, crony-capitalist economy, the State distributes surpluses to its vested interests (cronies) and transfers all the risk and consequences to the taxpayers.

Is this fair? The government doesn't really care; it rewards its favored constituencies, and transfers the costs and risk to everyone else. Those in government see this as their "job."

When we decide to spend money on something and forego investing it in something else, this is called "opportunity cost." Once the money is gone, we lost an opportunity to invest it elsewhere.

For example, suppose someone had to choose between buying a recreational vehicle and investing in Microsoft stock in 1986. If he chose to consume the money (buy the vehicle), by 2000 the vehicle was essentially worthless. If he invested the money in Microsoft, he was a millionaire by 2000.

He can't go back and choose the investment in Microsoft, nor can he make enough by working more hours to make up the lost opportunity. Spending/consuming rather than investing has enormous long-term consequences.

The State has no special wisdom; it collects the nation's surplus and distributes it to its favored constituencies. There is an opportunity cost to that spending.

In an open market, the opportunity costs are visible. The person who bought the recreational vehicle can see how much his vehicle depreciated, and the person who bought the Microsoft stock can see what it had gained in value.

The State can't account for the lost opportunities it has squandered in spending tomorrow's income today. It is myopic, and unable to look beyond the next election cycle. Those who are living in risk-free wonderlands funded and protected by the State complain if their share of the State income falls, and so the State responds by increasing the funding, even if it has to borrow the money.

The government has no mechanism for "pricing" risk and opportunity costs. Since it has no mechanism like an open market to price risk and opportunity costs, its decisions about where to distribute the nation's surpluses are blind to future consequences. When risk and consequence are mispriced, the decisions made will necessarily be uninformed ones. Uninformed decisions lead to disastrous results.

In this way, the government transfers the risk and consequences of its own decisions to the taxpayers. When they go bankrupt, so does the government.

You can't fool Mother Nature, you can't print oil, gold, wheat and iron, and you can't argue your way out a hole.

Ours is a "Pay As you Go" System

Many believe that the money they have paid into Social Security and Medicare over the decades is a form of insurance. They believe they paid their 'fair share" and therefore they deserve the benefits that have been promised.

This is based on a misunderstanding of the way our government programs work. Social Security and Medicare are "pay as you go" programs: all the money collected every year in Social Security and Medicare taxes is used to pay today's beneficiaries. The Federal government spends any leftover taxes on other things, and issues the Social Security Administration a worthless IOU for the leftover taxes it spent on other programs.

These worthless IOUs pile up in a bogus "Trust Fund" that contains no money. How do we know they are worthless? Let's say the Social Security Administration runs a deficit of $100 million one year, meaning it paid out $100 million more than it collected in taxes from current workers. It hands its IOU to the Treasury. Where does the Treasury get the $100 million? It sells $100 million in Treasury bonds to investors. It then gives the SSA the $100 million. In other words, the Treasury sold debt to raise the $100 million.

Now let's say the Pentagon needs $100 million more to fund its programs. Does it hand the Treasury an IOU? No. Where does the Treasury get the $100 million? It sells $100 million in Treasury bonds to investors, and then gives the Pentagon the $100 million.

You see the point: the IOU is worthless because it's funded by the sale of Treasury debt to investors, just like the rest of the government deficit.

There is no Trust Fund. All our Social Security taxes are spent immediately. This is called "pay as you go." This was not a problem back in 1950, when there were 16 workers for every retiree. But now that there are less than two workers per retiree, the system is unsustainable.

Remember the Medicare analysis? We pay in $30,000 over thirty years and want to take out $300,000 in our last fifteen years. That ratio only works if there are five workers for each beneficiary. There are now roughly two full-time workers for every beneficiary. The math simply doesn't work.

"Pay as you go" works fine when the economic tide is rising, but when it's ebbing then the current batch of workers don't pay enough taxes to fund the large pool of retirees and beneficiaries. The government has to pay the benefits with debt, and eventually those debts become large enough to crush the government's ability to borrow more.

The Tragedy of the Commons

Garrett Hardin's classic essay, *The Tragedy of the Commons* (1968), describes what happens when the self-interest of each individual is served by exploiting the public commons for their individual gain. When everyone sees the commons as "free for the taking," then the commons is soon destroyed for all.

In other words, the benefits of exploiting the freely available community resources (air, water, grazing land, etc.) are outsized to the individual, but ultimately catastrophic to everyone when the common resources are destroyed by overuse.

Since government tax revenue is a form of public commons, draining that resource to serve individual gain leads to the loss of the commons, as well as the loss of any notion of the "common good."

Self-interest is often distorted or short-sighted, and personal gain trumps the shared environment every time.

Since nothing is actually "free," the Tragedy of the Commons also describes the failure of the market to price shared assets, i.e. "the commons." The common environment—the air, rivers, etc. —can be squandered privately because there is no cost to individuals consuming those resources. The cost to the shared environment is called "external costs" because they are not reflected in the price of product or the manufacturers' expenses.

A classic example is a factory that dumps its industrial wastes into a river, destroying the fish and wildlife and ruining the water for human consumption. The cost to the environment (and to everyone who once derived value from the river) is very high, but it costs the factory owners nothing and is not added to the final price of the product. In this way, the "common good" is ignored by the marketplace.

Let's take a bikeway as an example. What is the market value of a bikeway? It can't be priced because the market doesn't recognize any value in the benefits it provides to the entire community: the reduction in air pollution, the improved health and lower future healthcare costs, the improved mental health of the bicyclists (endorphins flowing from exercise, reduced fatigue and depression, etc.) , the conservation of petroleum for better uses, the reduced traffic, the time saved not sitting in traffic, the reduction of energy needed to build more cars and trucks—all of these benefits are ignored by the market because they can't be priced.

The bikeway serves everyone, even those who don't use it, because it reduces vehicle traffic and improves the health of those using it which lowers the community's health costs. Yet it has no market value. This explains why the market cannot solve all problems in the economy and society: if the benefits to the community can't be priced, then the market doesn't recognize them. If the "downstream" costs are shifted to the commons, they are also not included in the market price.

Government benefits are like the Commons. Everyone serves their self-interest by grabbing as much as they can, and that pursuit of self-interest eventually destroys the Commons for everyone.

Our society is based on the fantasy that the unbridled pursuit of self-interest will magically lead to an optimum economy and society. What it leads to is a broken economy and society.

Moral Rot and the Tragedy of the Commons

When everyone is focused on "getting what's mine" without regard for the consequences to the commons, moral rot sets in as people justify lying, fraud, manipulating data, bribery, cheating and abuse of power to ensure they "get their fair share." As we have seen, moral rot has been normalized in today's power structure: super-wealthy financiers and corporations buy influence and effectively partner with the political aristocracy to establish "shadow systems" of finance and governance.

Rather than reject this corrupt neofeudal system, non-Elites remain quiet as long as they get a slice of the largesse. This complicity may require "gaming the system" or fudging the truth, but visibly corrupt Elites have lowered the moral standard to the point that non-Elites feel justified in pursuing their own "maximize my gain, minimize my contribution" strategy.

In this way, the moral rot at the top infects the entire economy and culture. The honest are effectively penalized and abusers of power are rewarded. Once no one is interested in what's happening to the commons, the commons collapse and everyone's slice of the wealth vanishes along with it.

The Paradox of Individual Honesty and Institutional Moral Rot

The moral rot has infected institutions, which are increasingly rewarding unethical "fudging" behavior and punishing integrity. Outside auditors, for example, are pressured to approve accounting reports that misrepresent assets and liabilities in subtle "gray area" ways.

Employees are pressured to approve shoddy products, lest they be fired for "not getting with the program." Government employees are pressured to investigate political enemies and whitewash investigations of powerful financial institutions. Faced with these kinds of indirect demands within institutions, basically honest people are subverted.

This subversion of individual integrity sets up a paradox: the majority of Americans are honest in their personal transactions, but they engage in dodgy "fudging" of ethics and integrity once they are in an institutional setting where the consequences of maintaining integrity are high: demotion, blacklisting, loss of job, etc.

As America has squandered more and more of its surplus on malinvestment, friction and interest on rising debt, opportunities to get ahead have also diminished along with productive investments. People become more willing to sacrifice their integrity "to get ahead": students cheat to improve their chances of getting into an Ivy league university, mortgage applicants "fudge" their income, job applicants exaggerate their qualifications, those seeking permanent disability exaggerate ailments and pain, and so on.

As individual and institutional integrity erodes, trust in institutions, data and standards of behavior all erode, too. Once trust in institutions decays, social cohesion is lost.

The Fruitless Search for Scapegoats

Unfortunately it is human nature to seek out scapegoats when things fall apart: foreign enemies and minorities are favorite targets of regimes seeking to escape responsibility for their own failures.

As things get worse, it will be tempting to seek scapegoats. How about bankers and wealthy Elites? We have to remember that these individuals simply did what everyone else did, which is pursue their own self-interest without regard for society as a whole. They were offered incentives to bribe politicians, so they did, and their wealth grew accordingly. This enabled them to offer even larger bribes and so their power increased.

As Jesus said, "He who is without sin among you, let him be the first to cast a stone at her."

Let's focus on our broken system, not corrupt individuals who took advantage of the broken system. As French economist Frederic Bastiat observed: "When plunder becomes a way of life for a group of men in a society, over the course of time they create for themselves a legal system that authorizes it and a moral code that glorifies it."

That is our nation today. We must change both the legal code and the moral code, and protect the commons that we all share.

The Proper Role of Government

I have tried to describe what happens when the Central Government controls the economy and society: it becomes an easy target for those seeking to enrich themselves by influencing government policy and regulation. The only solution is to limit and diffuse the power of government.

There is a proper role for a strong central government: to protect the civil liberties of the citizenry, protect the nation from foreign entanglements and enemies, and protect the nation's commons from individual or corporate exploitation.

The Founding Fathers established a strong but strictly limited Central Government to accomplish these critical tasks. Now the Central State has morphed into a Savior State that renders everyone dependent on its power to collect, borrow and redistribute money. We have traded liberty and community for the false security of an all-powerful Central State. What happens when that all-powerful government collapses under its own weight, complexity and corruption? To most Americans, that is "impossible." But as we have seen, over-indebtedness destroys not just households and companies; it eventually crushes national governments as well. In many ways, America is like the Roman Empire in its waning days: apparently permanent, but actually on the verge of collapse.

Virtually no one in 1985 thought the mighty, all-powerful government of the Soviet Union would ever crumble, yet it collapsed less than five years later.

Humans are not very good at predicting the future. We assume the present will continue on unchanged. Systems that are rotten at the core are like diseased trees; they look "healthy" until a stiff wind arises. When the tree crashes to the forest floor we're surprised because it appeared strong.

The financial/political system of America is like that tree, rotten at the core even as it appears "healthy" to the uninformed observer.

The proper role of government is to do *only those things that it alone can do*, and that boils down to a very few things: defense of the homeland, enforcement of civil liberties, protect citizens from exploitation and oppression by the State or private powers, protect minorities from the tyranny of majorities, protect the nation's commons from despoliation and maintain a level playing field for citizens to exercise their rights to life, liberty and the pursuit of happiness.

Centralization Leads to Corruption and Collapse

The concentration of wealth and power in centralized finance and government is a key dynamic in history. Increasing centralization offers benefits of efficiency until it reaches the point of diminishing return— what we will later call the top of the S-curve. Once centralization no longer offers broad efficiencies, it becomes a mechanism for concentrating wealth and power. In the normal course of capitalism, this inefficient entity would be replaced by more efficient enterprises and systems.

But the centralized entity has become so powerful that it won't allow itself to be replaced in capitalism's natural process of "creative destruction." Instead it protects its entrenched vested interests, who enrich themselves with predation, malinvestment and subsidies—all the hallmarks of unproductive crony capitalism.

The unproductive centralized entity increasingly poaches off the remaining productive sectors to fund its inefficiencies, eventually bleeding them dry. The entire Status Quo then collapses.

This is the essential dynamic behind the stagnation of all centralized economies, be they crony-capitalist, socialist or Communist. Beneath the surface label they are identical.

We will explore the negative consequences of centralization in more depth later.

Do We Have What It Takes to Get from Here to There?

Since I paid my way through college working for a building contractor, and later became a builder myself, I often visualize long-term projects as analogous to building a house: each step of the process must be completed before the next can begin, and a different set of tools, skills and experience is needed to complete each step. A person may have the desire to build a house, and the raw intelligence to do so, but these are insufficient to get the job done. First they must acquire the tools, skills, experience and capital.

We can phrase this basic question of any project in this way: do we have what it takes to get from here to there, that is, from where we are now to our goal?

In terms of an economy or society, we can ask a similar question: does this economy/society have what it takes to reach the next level of development and prosperity? Many times the answer is no, even though the nation is blessed with abundant natural resources, a motivated populace and other advantages.

In other cases, a nation like Japan has few natural resources, little arable land and relatively recent exposure to modern technology and capitalism, as it only opened its borders to the West in 1868. Democracy is also a late arrival to Japan; after the U.S. defeated the Japanese Empire in 1945, the United States imposed Western-style democracy on Japan.

Despite limited resources, total defeat and an unfamiliar form of government, Japan developed the world's second largest economy and widespread prosperity within a few decades. Recently, it has fallen into what I call a zombie economy, where the standard of living declines for most people while the political-financial Status Quo bleeds the nation dry to avoid imposing losses on its banks.

Clearly, Japan had what it took to develop rapidly from an impoverished agrarian backwater to an industrial powerhouse and from a closed feudal society to a constitutional democracy with a free press. But does Japan have what it takes to move beyond a centralized, bank-dominated zombie economy? Clearly it does not, as it has stagnated for over 20 years.

We can ask the same question of China, the European Union and the U.S.: do they have what it takes to move beyond unsustainable models of prosperity?

A certain sets of skills, knowledge and capital will take an individual, household, enterprise and nation to a certain level; beyond that, the tools available are simply not up to the task.

For example, societies without true rule of law have trouble developing new technologies, as individuals' innovations are stolen or copied before they can profit the developers; the absence of rule of law and protection of intellectual property places severe l limits on these economies' ability to create and reward new technologies. As a result, those individuals with the best ideas move to countries where they can profit from their innovations.

Economies that have come to depend on debt for their growth (a group that includes all the major economies) cannot overcome diminishing returns on debt; the more debt they create, the lower the yield on that debt.

Democracies where bailouts, tax breaks, subsidies and loopholes are all for sale end up with a dysfunctional, corrupt government and a zombie crony-capitalist economy dominated by wealthy individuals, banks and corporations.

Nations with low social mobility find their most ambitious citizens leave as soon as possible for countries where there are fewer social impediments and fewer "glass ceilings" to their aspirations and talents.

The desire for prosperity is not enough; for an economy and society to succeed, much more is needed.

Many observers have tried to establish why some cultures and nations become prosperous while other cultures and nations with equal natural resources never rise above a neofeudal economy in which a small Elite controls most of the wealth and everyone else is powerless and mired in poverty.

We can identify a short of list of key attributes that are necessary to get from widespread poverty to widespread prosperity:

1. The nation-state must secure the nation's territorial integrity. In other words, borders must be protected from invasion or intrusion and the land is under the control of the central government.

2. The nation-state provides the population with basic security (life, liberty, freedom from private or state oppression, freedom of speech, movement, enterprise and religion) and enforces a judicial system based on the rule of law, i.e. everyone is treated equally by the law and law enforcement.

3. The nation-state maintains the means to distribute sufficient food and energy to the entire population.

4. The nation-state allows the free expression of the population's values and interests.

5. The nation-state provides and protects individual rights to property, both real and intellectual.

6. The nation-state protects the common good.

7. The processes of governance are transparent and participatory.

8. The capital markets are transparent and the price of debt, risk and valuation are all discovered by the open market.

9. Centralization is limited by decentralization, competition, transparency and the community.

Any nation without all these attributes eventually runs into a barrier, and is unable to proceed to the next level of development, regardless of the type of government (socialist, communist, or capitalist) or the talents and skills of individual citizens.

These basic institutional qualities are like the foundation, walls and roof of a house; if any of these attributes is missing, the house cannot be completed.

In an enterprise, the qualities that got it to the start-up phase are not enough to enable fast growth. History is filled with promising enterprises that failed because they did not have sufficient capital and the necessary organizational production, marketing and management skills to expand.

In some cases, the very attributes that enabled initial success become obstacles to future growth.

If an individual wants to succeed in a trade, he/she must serve a lengthy apprenticeship that provides a foundation of all the necessary knowledge and a mastery of the tradecraft's essential skills. Capital (money) and desire are not enough.

Positions and titles can be bought with bribes; mastery cannot. This is a critically important reason why deeply corrupt cultures and economies cannot achieve widespread prosperity. If institutional positions can be bought, there is no reward for competence. Without competence, the institution fails. When enough critical institutions fail, the nation-state fails.

Many analysts seek to quantify what it takes to create widespread prosperity, and so they focus on attributes such as rule of law, demographics (a youthful population), the abundance of natural resources, and so on. But there are two other qualities that cannot be quantified: the values held by the populace and the intellectual framework that supports the entire edifice of government, marketplace and community.

If we take America as an example, early 20th-century sociologists such as Max Weber suggested that the Protestant work ethic was a key factor in capitalism's rapid expansion of wealth in Northern Europe and America. Though they do not have Christian cultural roots, the East Asian cultures of China, Korea and Japan also have a very strong work ethic.

As for an intellectual framework, America is blessed with a Constitution that embodies and expresses a very powerful understanding of human rights, limited government, liberty and justice. The Founding Fathers built upon the sturdy foundations of English common law, developed over centuries of experience, and the principles identified by the Enlightenment philosophers of England and France.

In East Asia, Confucian doctrines and values form the intellectual framework: respect for authority and elders, meritocracy within institutions and the primacy of the family unit. These values enabled China's rise to great power and achievement over the past two thousand years ago more recently over the past 30 years.

There are three parts to prosperity: positive values, an intellectual framework and the practical qualities listed above: territorial integrity, transparency, rule of law, and so on.

America has been deeply corrupted by financialization and centralization, which have undermined its values, intellectual framework and rule of law. Shadow systems of governance have replaced transparent government, and shadow systems of banking and finance have replaced open markets.

Financialization and centralization have created structural impediments to widespread prosperity. All of the positive characteristics we still have are not enough; we must regain all the qualities listed above.

Right now, our economy and society are dominated by parasitic concentrations of wealth and power. As a result, we don't have what it takes to get from here—centralized stagnation—to there: decentralized, transparent, sustainable systems open to all.

Section Three:
Structural Problems in our Economy and Society

Let's say we could wave a magic wand and get rid of fraud in our financial system. While we're at it, we also eliminate the worst excesses of crony capitalism and the neofeudal financial Aristocracy.

Is America now free of its long-term problems? Unfortunately, no; most of the truly critical problems are independent of the financial system. Fixing them will require a complete transformation of our society and economy.

Demographics: More Retirees, Fewer Workers

There's a saying: demographics is destiny. What this means is that a nation's path is ultimately defined not by politics, finance or social issues but by its demographics: the size and makeup of its generations. Nations with an aging population lose their vitality as the workforce dwindles and more of the nation's resources are spent on the elderly rather than on investment in the future.

Every country has what's called a "social contract" between the government and its citizens. In the modern, industrialized democracies, the social contract includes the explicit promise of generous pensions and healthcare benefits to everyone when they retire. In some countries, the retirement age is 55, in others it is 60 or 65. Since the average lifespan in advanced nations is close to 80 years, that means that retirees are drawing pension and healthcare benefits from the government for as long as 25 years.

As we have already seen, the average full-time worker in the U.S. pays around $35,000 into the Medicare system in a lifetime of work but extracts $350,000 to $500,000 in benefits from the system. Since Social Security and Medicare are "pay as you go" programs, benefits paid to current retirees are funded by taxes paid by current workers.

Here are the facts. In 2012, 57 million are drawing Social Security benefits, and Medicare pays all but a fraction of the healthcare expenses of 47 million retirees. There are about 112 million full-time workers and 38 million part-time workers who earn $10,000 or less annually. Since low-paid part-time workers pay very modest payroll taxes, the vast majority of payroll taxes are paid by full-time employees.

This means that the worker-retiree ratio is about 2-to-1: there are only two full-time workers for every retiree/beneficiary. This is a problem because the system was designed for a much higher worker-retiree ratio. If the average full-time worker earns $40,000 a year, and the average retiree extracts $40,000 in Social Security and Medicare benefits every year, the workers would have to pay 50% of their income in taxes to fund the benefits paid.

There are endless complexities in this issue; corporations pay taxes, too, and not every retiree receives the average benefit. But none of these factors change the big picture, which is no society can sustain a full-time worker-to-retiree ratio of 2-to-1, and this is ratio in most developed economies.

As standards of living and education rise, women tend to bear fewer children. This is true across all nations, ethnicities and populations. Birth rates are usually stated as the number of live births per woman over her lifetime. Since there are roughly equal numbers of males and females (unless cultural factors skew the ratio), then a ratio of 2.0 is considered the "replacement rate:" if each woman has two children in her lifetime, they replace the mother and father and the population remains stable.

In the U.S. , the birth rate is 2.1, slightly above the replacement rate. Add in the growth from immigration, and the population of the U.S. rises every year. In other countries, the birth rate is under replacement, which means that over time the population will decline unless it is offset with immigration.

As a nation's birth rate declines, the population of the nation ages. There are fewer young people entering the work force and more people retiring. The size of each generation matters. Many countries experienced a baby Boom after World War II, and that large cohort (roughly 75 million people in the U.S. born between 1946 and 1964) moves through the demographic chart like "a pig in a python," dominating the generations before and after with its sheer mass.

A large generation retiring has many consequences. As this generation needs money to fund retirement and healthcare, it sells its assets such as homes and stocks, putting pressure on the market value of those assets. As the Baby Boom generation stops working and paying taxes, tax revenues decline right when the retirees' start claiming their pensions and entitlements, dramatically increasing government spending.

In the U.S., 10,000 Baby Boomers start collecting Social Security and Medicare benefits every day, and this number will increase until about 2020 and then stay at that annual rate until 2029.

If the retiring generation refuses to trim their entitlements, taxes must rise for younger workers or government borrowing must increase. Since all government borrowing is essentially borrowing from future generations, this rising inequality fuels inequality and social conflict.

Demographics are destiny for the simple reason that the problems posed by an aging population cannot be solved with modest tax increases or other policies that work only at the margins. There are simply too many retirees and too few workers.

This demographic problem has been described in many books, such as *Fewer: How the New Demography of Depopulation Will Shape Our Future, While America Aged: the Next Financial Crisis* and *The Coming Generational Storm: What You Need to Know about America's Economic Future.*

The Status Quo "solution" is to "grow our way out of debt," but this no longer works when tax revenues are stagnant, debt payments are rising and the borrowed money has been squandered on malinvestment, friction and fraud.

The Decline of Paid Work

We all know technology eliminates jobs as robots and automation create labor-saving means of production that boost productivity. In general terms, the first Industrial Revolution was based on railroads, coal and steam power and the second Industrial Revolution arose from assembly lines powered by oil and electricity. The post-industrial third revolution was based on telecommunication, marketing and broadcast media (the telegraph, radio and television) and the fourth revolution has been driven by robotics, desktop fabrication, networked computers, software and the Internet.

Each revolution increased productivity which then increased prosperity. As manufacturing jobs were replaced by machines, the service industry expanded, creating more jobs than were lost to mechanization.

Optimists believe that this trend will continue: technology eliminates some jobs but creates even more employment as rising productivity generates more wealth. This extrapolation of past trends may be misguided, however, as the productivity gains resulting from software and the world wide web are slashing far more jobs than they are creating.

Consider a short list of entire sectors that have been decimated by automated "back office" web-based software and online shopping: music stores, book stores, travel agencies, newspaper classified ads and retail clerks displaced by self-service scanning. The jobs created for software engineers and staffers in online retailer warehouses are far fewer than those eliminated.

Networked knowledge-based software is eroding employment in standard white-collar sectors such as accounting, sales and marketing and even programming, as software enables each "knowledge worker" to be much more productive. Just a few years ago, each division within a corporation had a large IT (information technology) department. "Smart" integrated software and "cloud" computing is enabling a few workers to do what recently required a dozen employees.

Where mid-level managers once had an administrative assistant, now there may be one assistant for a half-dozen managers.

Blue-collar jobs are not immune to technology. The conventional trash collection truck once had a crew of three; now it only needs one, the driver, who picks up and empties curbside trash bins with a mechanical arm.

What drives this relentless reduction of labor? Labor is often the most expensive component, and so it stands out as the area that offers the most opportunities for increasing productivity and lowering costs.

Why are labor costs rising? One reason is that the healthcare system in the U.S. costs twice as much as comparable systems in competing advanced democracies such as Japan. The U.S. system demonstrably delivers less effective care to the populace than systems that cost 50% less. The U.S. system spends 50% of our healthcare spending on fraud, friction, defensive medicine and malinvestment. This is a $1 trillion "tax" on labor in the U.S., as it makes labor far more expensive to employers in the U.S. than it does to employers in other advanced economies.

Another factor is that technology continually gets cheaper and more productive while labor keeps getting more costly.

Even demographics play a part. As the population ages, the costs of Social Security and Medicare rise, and so payroll taxes rise, too. A few decades ago, the employer and employee paid 3% of the employee's wage in Social Security taxes. Now the total is 15.3%.

Technology can't be stopped. Once something is faster, better, cheaper, people will gravitate to it.

How about offshoring and globalization? Hasn't that hurt employment in the U.S.? Clearly, the U.S. could and should do more to create incentives for businesses to keep production "at home;" after all, competing nations such as Japan and Germany have policies that support small manufacturing firms and encourage them to keep production in the home country.

But globalization is much more than offshoring manufacturing. Companies like IBM, McDonalds and Apple do more business overseas than they do in the U.S.; most large U.S. corporations earn between half and two-thirds of their revenues overseas. The job growth in these companies occurs where the company is growing revenues, and that is mostly overseas in fast-growing emerging economies. It isn't realistic to expect companies to keep most of their jobs in the U.S. when the majority of their sales and customers are six time zones away.

If you have employees in one country who do the same work as your U.S. employees for one-third the cost, when you need to hire more people, where will you hire them? The difference in wages globally is called "wage arbitrage," and it is a thorny issue for every advanced economy that has much higher labor costs and taxes than developing economies.

Small business in the U.S. has many incentives to lower labor costs. Taxes and fees are rising every year as local governments seek to increase their revenue, and healthcare insurance for an older worker or an employee with children can be 50% or more of the worker's salary. Competition is fierce and revenues are always under pressure. The only way to survive for many small enterprises is to invest in technology that increases productivity at the expense of labor.

My own modest enterprise is only financially feasible because software that once cost thousands of dollars to develop is now either free or low-cost. The "on-demand" model for publishing my books means the physical book is only printed when a customer orders a copy. There is no costly shipping to distributors who then return unsold copies to be pulped. The formatting and pre-production of the book is free; it is all done automatically online. Two-thirds of my sales are digital e-books that are delivered to customers via the web. All the marketing, accounting of sales and royalties are automated and available online. I do my tax returns with inexpensive software and pay my quarterly estimated state taxes online.

Many other small enterprises have the same experience. We're only able to make a living because the back office complexities have become cheap and simple enough that we can do the work ourselves.

Many people do not understand the pressure on companies to maintain profits while revenues remain flat. Once local government tax revenues decline, government agencies are also under pressure to raise productivity and lower labor costs, which are generally three-quarters of government budgets.

There are two basic reasons why employment surged in the 1990s and 2000s. In the 1990s, the Internet revolution generated an investment boom much like the railroad boom of the 1870s. Money was invested in all sorts of schemes and ideas, and many did not pan out. Once the infrastructure was in place, the boom turned to a bust as unproductive businesses foundered and jobs were eliminated.

When the Federal Reserve responded to the dot-com bust of 2000 with super-low interest rates, that policy triggered a housing bubble that was at heart a credit bubble: anyone with a pulse could obtain a mortgage and speculate in the housing market. People bought multiple houses with "liar loans" (no-document mortgages) and "flipped" them for short-term profits. Millions of jobs were created in the mortgage service industry, home building, furnishing sales, and so on. As house prices skyrocketed, homeowners extracted their equity with home equity lines of credit (HELOCs) and spent the proceeds on vacations, boats, home improvement projects and consumer goods.

When the bubble popped, these jobs disappeared.

The same can be said of the millions of jobs that have been eliminated by technology: they aren't coming back, and the jobs created in the software and Internet fields are not only much fewer in number than the jobs lost, they are also under relentless pressure as programming is itself increasingly automated.

Author Jeremy Rifkin has discussed many of these trends in his book *The End of Work*. It is not a message we want to hear because it poses a problem that cannot be solved with more education. We can graduate 100,000 PhDs in biochemistry but that doesn't automatically create 100,000 jobs in bioscience. Many people hope that emerging technologies such as biotechnology and nanotechnology will create new industries on the scale of the Internet, but not every new technology creates millions of new jobs. If we know anything about technology, it is that it constantly becomes faster, better and cheaper, and that it does so largely by eliminating human labor.

From one perspective, business is able to charge a premium based on customer ignorance. An airline can charge a premium for a seat on a flight because the customer doesn't know what other seats on competing flights cost. Once the customer knows, the company's ability to charge a premium for its secret knowledge disappears.

A similar trend is apparent in the online supply chain. What was once scarce in a locale (a muffler for an aging vehicle, for example) is now plentiful online, and as a result the local supplier is unable to charge a premium based on scarcity.

The barriers to entry—the cost of starting a business—have also plummeted, removing a key advantage once held by large businesses. The cost of the machinery was so prohibitive, only a large, well-capitalized business could afford to own and operate the equipment. Consider recording and editing music. The equipment cost many thousands of dollars, and so record companies had a monopoly on recording and distributing musical recordings. Now any aspiring musician can produce a professional-quality recording with software that costs a few hundred dollars and distribute the recording via the web at an extremely low cost.

In industry after industry, the foundation of their business model has been undermined. To survive, they have to adapt technologies that radically lower the cost structure of their business. The alternative is to go out of business.

America has long welcomed immigrants as a dynamic source of labor and energy. America continues to attract immigrants who understand that the U.S. is despite its many problems still the land of opportunity. This influx of motivated workers means there is a surplus of labor. Labor is like any other part of the economy: it is priced by supply and demand. If there is one job and ten available workers, the competition for the scarce job keeps the wage low. We have minimum wage laws to keep workers from being exploited, but supply and demand still affect the price of goods and labor alike.

Labor can only charge a premium if the skillset is scarce and the demand is high. Education is not necessarily a panacea. If there are ten qualified PhDs for every university professorship that opens up, the salary of professors will eventually respond to supply and demand.

In every sector of the economy, the premium charged by "middle men" is disappearing, and so are the jobs in the middle between customer and supplier. Technologies such as 3-D printing and software development tools are still in their infancy, and as they spread through the economy they will disrupt more and more business models and eliminate premiums that have been taken for granted.

The more powerful and interactive the technologies are, the faster the rate of change. That is our world.

Technological change tends to spread throughout the private sector before it reaches the monopolies of government and government-supported cartels such as healthcare and education. Government is a monopoly because it has a monopoly on coercion, taxation and selling Treasury bonds to fund deficit spending. Government ignores the marketplace of price because it can spend as much as it wants by either raising taxes or borrowing more money. But as we have explained in previous chapters, there are limits on taxation and borrowing money: the government can "print" or borrow money, but it cannot "print" or create wealth (surplus).

Once you start living on borrowed money, you are borrowing from future generations, and this only works for a short period of time when the economy is declining for structural reasons.

This explains why the healthcare, education and other government service sectors dodged previous recessions, and why salaries and benefits for these sectors have remained generous in previous recessions: the government doesn't feel any supply-demand pressures, as it simply borrows more during recessions.

But government's ability to ignore price, supply and demand is eroding as tax revenues are declining and Federal borrowing has skyrocketed. The Elites expected this massive borrowing and spending to "grow our way out of recession" but for all the reasons we have covered here, that hasn't happened. All we're doing is saddling future taxpayers with crushing debts.

As a result, even the government and its protected sectors are feeling the pressure of market forces. College tuition and healthcare have both exploded higher, rising 600% in the past two decades while household income stagnated. This is simply not sustainable, and the healthcare and education sectors will soon experience the same reduction in labor costs that the private sector has already experienced.

The government was pleased to join in the financialization bubbles in stocks and housing because tax revenues rocketed higher. But those bubbles have burst and are not coming back. As a result, the government is now like the household borrowing 40% of its expenses every year—it is digging itself a hole it cannot escape from.

Eventually, all the government-protected sectors will have to cut labor costs just like the private sector.

The key point here is that faster, better, cheaper always wins. The government and private cartels can impose barriers that limit competition, but eventually the premium they can extract declines.

The second key point is that the industries of the fourth industrial revolution—robotics, desktop fabrication, networked computers, software and the Internet—are destroying more jobs than they create and destroying more protected premiums (profits) than they generate.

Process costs, labor costs and labor time per unit are all declining. Labor is in surplus and the ability to profit from ignorance and local scarcity is also declining.

As private-sector labor and profits decline, government tax revenues will also drop. Every enterprise, private or public, has a simple choice: either reduce costs to fit lower revenues, or create more premium. Borrowing money to maintain the Status Quo is just a form of self-destructive denial.

These issues are structural and cannot be "fixed" with policy changes. There are no easy fixes, and we cannot limit the spread of technology and innovation to protect jobs and profits without crippling the economy. Our only choice is to pursue adaptability and resilience and replace the failed models of governance and finance that are leading the nation over the cliff.

Why Privatizing Government Monopolies Is Not the Answer

Many people think that the best way to expose government services to market forces is to privatize them, i.e. contract them out to private enterprise. While this has surface appeal, it only creates a new set of unintended consequences and perverse incentives.

The problem with privatization is it only substitutes one monopoly for another monopoly. A private monopoly is even worse than a government monopoly, for the citizens have no say over the private monopoly. Simply handing a government service to a private contractor maintains the monopoly, which is the real problem. The only real solution is to break up monopolies with competition.

A brief story will help illustrate the difference between local government and of concentrated private capital.

Let's say a small community has abundant fresh-water resources. A large multinational corporation approaches the town council to purchase the rights to the water. The multi-billion dollar corporation seeking a monopoly presents what appears to be a windfall to the city leadership: new jobs, a new park, stable tax revenues, and so on.

But the city government is no match for a global corporation which possesses the great advantage of *information asymmetry*: the corporate leadership knows their own long-range plans to exploit the water monopoly while the city leaders know only what the corporate public-relations team decides to tell them.

Given the legal thickets of water rights and contractual laws, the global corporation can easily construct a *complexity fortress* that is essentially impenetrable to the inquiries of the city leadership.

If the corporation issues thousands of pages of documents, what information is actually available? Very little; the city doesn't have the resources to make sense of this legal *complexity fortress.*

Presented with what appears to be a windfall, the town leaders agree to sell the water rights to the corporation.

Very quickly, the power of private monopoly flashes its teeth: the company decides to renege on various employment and public improvement promises, citing "market conditions." The residents soon discover that ceding of their water rights is legally unbreakable but the promised dividends from the corporation are all rescindable without recourse.

The corporation, of course, has a veritable army of attorneys and consultants to defend its rights, while the township has very limited resources to defend its citizens from exploitation. The corporation has the wealth to influence higher government regulators to ignore the city and approve the corporation's actions.

While I have pointed out the inevitable implosion of State finances, this does not mean local or even national government is superfluous. It simply means that the "Savior State" that has become dependent on ever-rising debt and that has been captured by financial Elites will collapse. That doesn't mean private monopolies are the answer.

The answer is to increase competition and break up concentrations of power and monopoly in both public and private sectors. If the city trash collection service is high cost and uncompetitive, the solution is to enable competitors to enter the market, and to maintain an open market for this service. Charter schools are creating competition in public schools that were previously monopolies.

The profit motive has limits in terms of serving the community and protecting the commons. Consider the ill-advised movements to privatize local police forces and prisons. Once it becomes profitable to arrest and imprison citizens, then private police will naturally increase arrests and fill the private prisons to maximize profit, which is the only purpose of a private corporation.

There are perverse incentives to both narrow self-interest and monopoly. Both of these eventually lead to the destruction of the common good and the economy.

Diminishing Returns

I have mentioned diminishing returns as a key concept. This dynamic is also called marginal return. The basic idea is simple: if we need to invest more and more capital and energy to maintain the same output, our return on investment is diminishing. Another way to understand this is to think of a situation where adding 10% more investment yields a 100% increase in yield. One example is adding fertilizer to unproductive soil. The first 10% causes our harvest to double. The "low hanging fruit" of increased productivity has already been picked by this first application of fertilizer, however, so when we add 20% more the yield only rises 30%. As we keep adding more fertilizer, the yield drops significantly. Eventually, the increase is marginal: we're spending 50% more money and the yield is only 3% higher.

Here are two other examples. The topline U.S. fighter aircraft a few years ago was the F-18 Super Hornet, the latest version of which cost around $54 million each. The replacement aircraft, the F-35 Lightning, costs over $200 million each, $300 million each when research and development are included. The program has suffered major cost over-runs and some estimates of the aircraft's total lifecycle costs run as high as $600 million each. The F-35 is so costly that the U.S. Armed Services have significantly reduced the number of aircraft on order.

The F-35 appears to be unaffordable, even for the best-funded military on Earth.

Here is the question: is the F-35 four times more lethal than the F-18? Can it consistently shoot down four equivalents of the F-18 in air-to-air combat? If the U.S. can't afford to operate enough of these aircraft because they are so expensive, couldn't an enemy overwhelm the superiority of the F-35 with sheer numbers?

The point is that the returns on investing six times more money per aircraft appear marginal; we're not getting an aircraft that's six times better. It may well be that no aircraft could be six times better than the already capable F-18. The cost has climbed to the point that we cannot even afford to buy the desired number of planes. That in itself is diminishing returns.

As I have noted before, the U.S. healthcare system costs roughly twice as much as the universal systems of our advanced-economy competitors. Yet studies have found U.S. care does not yield longer lifespans or lower death rates from chronic diseases. In some metrics of healthcare results, the U.S. ranks near the bottom in the list of 50 developed economies. Clearly, we are not getting any return at all for spending twice as much as competing nations.

There is an opportunity cost to these kinds of marginal return investments. What else could the nation buy with the $1.35 trillion we waste on fraud, friction, defensive medicine and malinvestments in healthcare? What other defense systems could we buy of we held the cost of new aircraft to only double the cost of the F-18 ($100 million each) instead of $300 million each?

When there is no pressure from competition and market forces, costs quickly rise and diminishing returns set in. When vested interests rule the budget, effectiveness is set aside in favor of cronyism.

Cartels and monopolies maximize their profits by rigging prices and keeping costs elevated.

All of these forces of marginal return are active in the Central State crony capitalism that dominates our economy. The Central State has no competition, and so it has no pressure to control costs or become more productive or efficient.

The point here is that we receive no real return on investment when diminishing returns take hold. Trillions of dollars are invested but there is precious little yield on that stupendous investment. Vested interests receive their slice of the national income, but what do the citizenry get? What else could have been funded with the money that was squandered on fraud, friction and malinvestment?

Right now we don't have to answer those questions because we're borrowing over a $1 trillion a year to fund all the marginal-return programs. These immense sums are not improving the economy or society; they are depriving the nation of scarce capital and resources that could have been invested wisely and productively elsewhere.

No wonder our economy is stagnating. We refuse to make adult trade-offs and instead borrow enough to fund every malinvestment, every cartel and every source of friction.

Since our children and grandchildren will have to pay interest on our massive debt for their entire lives, it is criminal to borrow and spend money that yields essentially zero return on investment.

The End of Cheap Energy and EROEI

Many people think "peak oil" is about the world is "running out of oil." Actually, "peak oil" is about the world running out of cheap, easy-to-get oil.

The abundance or scarcity of energy is only one factor in its price. As the cost of extraction, transport, refining, and taxes rise, so does the "cost basis" or the total cost of production from the field to the pump. Anyone selling oil below its cost basis will lose money and go out of business.

We are trained to think that anything that is abundant will be cheap, but energy is a special case: it can be abundant but costly, because it's become costly to produce.

EROEI (energy returned on energy invested) helps illuminate this point. In the good old days, one barrel of oil invested might yield 100 barrels of oil extracted and refined for delivery. Now it takes one barrel of oil to extract and refine 5 barrels of oil, or perhaps as little as 3 barrels of unconventional or deep sea oil.

In the old days, oil would shoot out of the ground once a hole was drilled down to the deposit. All the easy-to-find, easy-to-get oil has been consumed; now even Saudi Arabia must pump millions of gallons of water into its wells to push the oil up out of the ground. Recent discoveries of oil are in costly locales deep offshore or in extreme conditions. It takes billions of dollars to erect the platforms and wells to reach the oil, so the cost basis of this new oil is high.

It doesn't matter how abundant oil might be; it's the cost that impacts the economy. High energy costs mean households must spend more of their income on energy, leaving less for everything else. High energy costs act as a hidden "tax" on the economy, raising the price of everything that uses energy.

As household incomes drop and vehicles become more efficient, demand for gasoline declines. Normally, we would expect lower demand to lead to lower prices. But since the production costs of oil have risen, there is a "floor" for the price of gasoline. As EROEI drops, the price floor rises, regardless of demand.

This decrease in real incomes and ratcheting-higher energy costs could lead to a situation where energy is abundant but few can afford to buy much of it.

The U.S. has two abundant sources of fossil energy: coal and natural gas, which are typically used to generate electricity and fuel households with gas appliances. Transportation requires liquid fuels such as gasoline and jet fuel. While vehicles can be modified to burn natural gas rather than diesel or gasoline, this requires a major investment were the U.S. to switch a major portion of its 250-million vehicle fleet from gasoline to natural gas. In other words, the transition to another fossil fuel would not be cheap or quick.

Coal can be transformed into liquid fuel, but the process is not cheap or easy. The point is that any major transition to another form of hydrocarbon energy will be costly.

Energy, like grain and other exportable commodities, is set on the global market. That means that the price rises or falls depending on global demand and supply. Right now, natural gas is inexpensive because it is abundant in the U.S.   But were demand from overseas to increase significantly, gas producers would sell to the highest bidder, effectively pushing up prices in America as well.

If you look at the long-term chart of prices of essential commodities such as oil, natural gas and wheat, you will notice large swings in price. Geopolitics, global booms and busts, and currency fluctuations all impact the cost of oil and grain. But since every sector of the economy consumes energy, a steady rise in the cost of oil acts as a "tax" on the entire economy.

At some price point alternative energy sources become competitive with hydrocarbon energy: geothermal, wind, thermal solar, tidal and so on. These have the distinct advantage of being decentralized and domestic, i.e. not imported, and they are also clean sources of energy that don't pollute the air or water table.

But switching to alternative energy is costly, too, as it requires a major investment of capital. Capital (savings) is always scarce, and borrowing money adds the cost of interest.

The point is that switching from increasingly expensive oil to another energy source is costly, even when the energy source itself is "cheap" and abundant. (What can be cheaper and more abundant than sunshine, geothermal, the tides and wind?)

Experts measure the value of energy by its density, that is, how much energy it holds by volume or weight. Gasoline is a very high-density fuel, and it is also easily transportable. Coal is a lower-density fuel and less easily transportable because it takes more coal than gasoline by volume to provide the same amount of energy. Solar panels are low-density generators of energy, and so the electricity they generate must be collected into a grid or stored in a high-density battery.

The lower the energy-density of the energy source, the more you need to replace the high-density of gasoline.

We can summarize the key points in this way: "Easy-to-get oil was an almost-free lunch, but that almost-free lunch is gone. Now there is no free lunch, and energy will cost more." Gasifying coal is not cheap, converting 100 million vehicles to natural gas is not cheap, and solarizing the U.S. electrical grid is not cheap: the cheap energy solutions have been consumed, and what we're left with is a mix of higher cost sources and solutions. That means that a greater percentage of dwindling household incomes will go to paying higher energy costs.

Abundant energy does not necessarily mean cheap energy, especially in transportation. Those days are past. Since the global economy is dependent on cheap, easily transportable energy, that means slower growth as scarce capital must be invested in constructing new energy infrastructures.

There may be technical breakthroughs such as thorium reactors and "artificial photosynthesis," but once again these sources of energy will be costly to construct and will require capital to be diverted from consumption and other investments. There is no "free lunch" in energy except conservation, i.e. doing more with less energy, but even conservation requires some investment, if not of cash then of time and attention.

We can do much more with much less, and higher costs will drive conservation as the "cheapest" alternative. This will open new opportunities for enterprise, but the primary point remains: the era of dirt-cheap, easily transportable fuels is fading, and the cost basis of energy will inevitably rise.

Healthcare in Crisis

Healthcare in America is a prime example of diminishing returns: the more money we throw at healthcare, the slimmer the improvements in health. As I say in all my books: health is the ultimate wealth, because without health then the rest of one's wealth is meaningless. The skyrocketing cost and declining health of the citizenry are core problems, because it is clear that borrowing trillions of dollars to throw into healthcare is 1) not sustainable and 2) not yielding equivalent improvements in longevity and health.

The system is broken, but the problem is larger than just the broken healthcare system I call "sickcare" because it generates profits from illness and chronic disease, not from wellness or health. The low-hanging fruit of public health has been plucked, and the illnesses now plaguing America are complex "lifestyle" diseases such as diabesity that are not fixable with an antibiotic or other pill.

Our ill-health is not the result of a broken healthcare system—the American lifestyle generates ill-health. This is a complex problem that ties into many issues from the design of our cities (car-centric, not built for pleasant walking and bicycling), a market-driven worship of convenience (fast food, pills as cures, etc.) and a diet that has strayed far from healthy foods.

Our wealth is illusory if our physical and mental health continues deteriorating as a result of our lifestyle and culture. Borrowing and dumping more trillions into a broken system is not fixing the underlying problems. We already spend twice as much per person as other developed democracies, yet our national health is not improving, it is declining.

Is Questioning Illegitimate Authority a "Disease" or the Core of American Liberty?

One deeply disturbing trend in the U.S. that has gathered momentum since the September 11, 2001 terrorist attack is the erosion of fundamental civil liberties and the pathologizing of resistance to authority that may well be illegitimate.

Authoritarianism is unquestioning obedience to authority. It is deeply counter to the basic American values of independent thinking and moral judgment based on conscience. The American Revolution was the inevitable result of American colonists concluding that the authority of the British Crown was not just oppressive but illegitimate. In other words, the Crown's power to tax and restrict colonial commerce was legal but illegitimate.

How can authority be legal but illegitimate? The answer lies in the quote from Frederic Bastiat: *"When plunder becomes a way of life for a group of men in a society, over the course of time they create for themselves a legal system that authorizes it and a moral code that glorifies it."*

Those in power always construct a legal justification for their authority, and use the tools of propaganda and persuasion to legitimize their power with a false moral authority.

For example, Section 1021(b)(2) of the National Defense Authorization Act (NDAA), an act of Congress that annually funds the U.S. Armed Forces, authorized the military to detain U.S. citizens indefinitely, strip them of due process and hold them in military facilities, including offshore penal colonies.

The fact that this outright gutting of basic civil liberties was buried in the politically sacrosanct military funding budget reflects the authorities' desire to hide it from inquiry and public awareness.

Sure enough, when the section was struck down in Federal Court, the Administration claimed "the government has compelling arguments that it should be reversed."

Then there's the FISA Amendment Act, which retroactively makes legal what has traditionally been illegal under our Constitution— warrantless wiretapping, eavesdropping and monitoring of U.S. citizens.

Under the Obama administration, the Central State has staked out the "legal" grounds for total mobilization of the American populace and economy with the Orwellian-titled National Defense Resources Preparedness, an Executive Order filled with extralegal directives and vaguely defined over-reach.

While the Executive Order is legal, how can an order that grants essentially unlimited "emergency" Executive Powers without an act of Congress be legitimate under our Constitution?

Setting aside the many unanswered questions raised by 9/11, public documentation show that the problem was not so much an intelligence failure—officials in the FBI and CIA had identified the hijackers as "people of interest" and knew an attack was increasingly likely—as a failure of agency coordination fueled by top-level incompetence and complacency.

Rather than focus on improving inter-agency coordination, there has been a dramatic sea change in U.S. intelligence and law enforcement since 9/11. The focus has shifted from targeted intelligence gathering and investigation to establishing a domestic intelligence net that sifts all electronic data and communication for "suspicious" data. In other words, protecting "our way of life" is more important than civil liberties. This is of course an Orwellian reversal of what the Founding Fathers believed, which was that *civil liberties are our way of life*.

If we reckon there are perhaps 8,000 active terrorists in the entire world, the U.S. now fields 100 Federal employees for each terrorist. There are some 850,000 Americans with top secret clearance, which gives us a taste of the size of the national security state-within-a-state.

The danger of political activities being lumped in with criminal activity is higher than most Americans believe. We cannot say that it "can't happen here" because it is already happening here: the Espionage Act has been used to stifle whistleblowers who threatened to expose official malfeasance.

In other words, anyone questioning the Status Quo or exposing corruption becomes an "enemy of the State" who can be investigated without judicial oversight and pursued on a variety of trumped-up "national security" charges.

Questioning authority—the bedrock of American liberty—is increasingly viewed as threatening and/or illegal.

This has even seeped into mental health, and from there into schools and society. The Diagnostic and Statistical Manual of Mental Disorders (DSM) published by the American Psychiatric Association establishes the standardized criteria for classifying mental disorders.

One such classification—"oppositional defiant disorder" (ODD) — transforms anti-authoritarian individualism into a "disease," i.e. a pathology, that must be "treated" by those in authority—in this case, psychiatrists. The official symptoms of ODD include "often actively defies or refuses to comply with adult requests or rules" and "often argues with adults." Note this behavior is not that of unruly juvenile delinquents—that is called "conduct disorder."

More broadly, anyone who questions the legitimacy of authority in America is labeled as "having issues with authority."

Granted, refusing to comply with any and all authority may suggest some psychological difficulty, but questioning the legitimacy of authority is not pathology.

There are similar examples in the housing market, where people without any mortgage at all have been evicted by "too big to fail" banks claiming the owners defaulted on a mortgage that doesn't exist.

All of these examples reveal an America in which authority is above the law and free from public inquiry, while those who question the legitimacy of power grabs and illegal seizures are treated as criminals or marginalized as mentally ill.

This is of course precisely how authoritarian regimes suppress anyone questioning the legitimacy of their power.

The Cost of Stagnation:
Social Recession and Permanent Adolescence

What happens to the social fabric of an advanced nation after a decade or more of economic stagnation? For an answer, we can turn to Japan. The second-largest economy in the world has stagnated since its speculative bubbles in stock and real estate popped in 1990, and the consequences for the "lost generations" who have come of age in the "lost decades" have been dire. In many ways, the social conventions of Japan are unraveling under the relentless pressure of an economy in seemingly permanent decline.

Young people who have entered the workforce in the past two decades have faced diminishing opportunities. This has created not just financial insecurity, but social, cultural and psychological malaise.

The gap between extremes of income at the top and bottom of society has been growing in Japan for years; to the surprise of many outsiders, once-egalitarian Japan is becoming a nation of haves and have-nots.

The media in Japan have popularized the phrase *kakusa shakai*, literally meaning "gap society." As the elite slice of society prospers and younger workers are increasingly marginalized, the media has focused on the shrinking middle class.

Many young people have come to mistrust big corporations, having seen their fathers or uncles eased out of "lifetime" jobs in the relentless downsizing of the past twenty years. From the point of view of the younger generations, the loyalty their parents unstintingly offered to companies was wasted.

They have also come to see diminishing value in the grueling study and tortuous examinations required to compete for the elite jobs in academia, industry and government; with opportunities fading, long years of study are perceived as pointless.

Here are some characteristics of Japan's "social recession":

-- Once-egalitarian Japan is becoming a nation of haves and have-nots.

-- More than one-third of the workforce is part-time as companies have shed the famed Japanese lifetime employment system.

-- The slang word "freeter" combines the English "free" and the German "arbeiter" or worker; this describes workers who are free to move between jobs and often describes part-time workers. A typical "freeter" wage is 1,000 yen ($12.60) an hour at current dollar/yen exchange rates.

-- The Ministry of Health, Labor and Welfare estimates that 50 percent of high school graduates and 30 percent of college graduates now quit their jobs within three years of leaving school.

-- Japan's slump has lasted so long that a "New Lost Generation" is coming of age, joining Japan's first "Lost Generation" which graduated into the bleak job market of the 1990s.

-- These trends have led to an ironic moniker for the Freeter lifestyle: *Dame-Ren* (No Good People). The *Dame-Ren* (pronounced dah-may-ren) get by on odd jobs, low-cost living and drastically diminished expectations.

-- Many young men now reject the macho work ethic of their fathers and the traditional Samurai ideal of masculinity. Derisively called "herbivores" or "Grass-eaters," these young men are uncompetitive and uncommitted to work, evidence of their deep disillusionment with Japan's troubled economy.

-- These shifts have spawned a disconnect between genders so pervasive that Japan is experiencing a sharp decline in marriage, births, and even romance.

-- The trend of never leaving home has sparked an almost tragi-comical countertrend of Japanese parents who actively seek mates to marry off their "parasite single" offspring as the only way to get them out of the house.

-- An even more extreme social disorder is *Hikikomori*, or "acute social withdrawal," a condition in which the young live-at-home person will virtually wall themselves off from the world by never leaving their room.

Many young people in Japan are devotees of fantasy fashions, outlandish clothing sometimes based on fictional characters in *manga* or *anime* (Japanese comics and animated films). This fantasy world is an expression of extended adolescence forced on young adults facing truncated opportunities for adulthood (secure careers, marriage, family, homeownership) who are stuck in a kind of "suspended animation" between youth and adulthood.

It's as if there is a split in the road and no third way: some young people make it onto the traditional corporate or government career path, and everyone else is left in part-time suspended animation with few options for adult expression or development.

Young people have money and time to burn on outlandish costumes because few earn enough to have their own families or flats. They work part-time for low wages and live at home or in tiny one-room apartments. Few own cars because they 1) don't earn enough to support a car and 2) they're uninterested in acquiring status symbols or prestige signifiers.

This is not just a generational shift: it reflects a realistic understanding that opportunities for secure, high-paying employment have diminished over the past 20 years. There are plenty of low-level part-time jobs, but few with the guarantees that their parents took for granted.

Sound familiar? Social recession and extended adolescence are playing out in Europe and the U.S. as well.

Our economies and societies are still operating on a postwar model that no longer works. As a result, there are fewer paths to marriage, having children and home ownership. With opportunities shrinking, the only option for many is a debilitating permanent adolescence. We need a third way, and that's what the last section of the book is about.

The Contradictions of Consumerist Capitalism and the End of Growth

The model of capitalism adopted by advanced economies holds that consumerist demand creates wealth, prosperity and happiness. Since demand is endless, growth is also endless.

But as we have seen, this growth is increasingly dependent on debt and leverage, what we call financialization.

An economy dependent on debt-fueled consumption to power its "endless growth" is one that will eventually implode from its internal contradictions: debt and leverage eventually exceed the collateral and the national surplus, and the narcissism created by rampant consumerism leads to social recession, a crippling state of permanent adolescence and great personal frustration and unhappiness.

The ultimate contradiction in this debt-consumption version of capitalism is this: how can an economy have "endless growth" when wages and opportunities for secure, high-paying jobs are both declining? It cannot. Financialization, consumerist narcissism and the end of growth are inextricably linked.

Economic malaise leads to profound social recession that affects society, workplaces, families, individuals that then feeds back into the economic stagnation.

Definancialization is the process in which excessive speculation, debt and leverage reverse, crushing the economy with malinvestment and legacy debt while the crony-capitalist Central State attempts to stem the resulting deflation with massive Keynesian stimulus (fiscal deficits).

What we're seeing in Japan is the confluence of three dynamics: definancialization, the demise of growth-positive demographics and the devolution of the consumerist model of endless "demand" and "growth."

What consumerist excess actually creates are alienation, social atomization, narcissism, and a profound contradiction at the heart of the consumerist model of "growth": the narcissism that powers consumerist desire and identity is at odds with the demands of the workplace that generates the income needed to consume.

Narcissism is the result of the consumerist society's relentless focus on the essential credo of consumerism, which is "the only self that is real is the self that is purchased and projected." The coddled consumer has come to believe the world revolves around him/her.

The narcissism that results from this focus on personal gratification via consumption cripples the person in the workplace. The flattening of corporate management and the demands for higher productivity requires higher interpersonal skillsets, the very skills that have no place in consumerism.

The narcissism bred by consumerism has nurtured a brittle immaturity (permanent adolescence) that leaves many young people without the tools needed to handle criticism, collaboration and the pressures of the workplace.

If there is any personality that is unsuited for the demanding "New Normal" workplace, it is the narcissistic consumer—the very type of person that our consumption-dependent economy creates and nurtures. We can call this paradox a Cultural Contradiction of Capitalism.

Sociologist Daniel Bell's 1988 book, *The Cultural Contradictions of Capitalism*, brilliantly laid out the contradiction at the heart of all consumer-dependent cultures: capitalism harbors the seeds of its own downfall by creating a need for personal gratification via consumption and leisure that corrodes the work ethic that led to capitalism's success in the first place.

"Personal gratification" is the driver of narcissism and consumerism, two sides of the same coin. Consumerist marketing glorifies the "projected self" as the "true self," encouraging self-absorption even as it erodes authentic identity, self-esteem and the resilience which enables emotional growth—the essential characteristic of adulthood.

Globalization and Triffin's Paradox

For the most part, the concepts we've discussed so far are intuitive; for example, we all understand a household budget and a national budget share the same basic principles. The next topic is not so intuitive, and many people have difficulty understanding the dynamics and accepting the conclusions.

Let's start with the power to print paper money in the home country and exchange it for oil, steel, autos, furniture, etc. in other countries 5,000 miles away. On the face of it, we might ask why anyone should accept paper in exchange for real goods. After all, if someone prints money in their country, we don't accept it in trade for our oil. They must exchange their paper money for U.S. dollars first.

There is only one country that gets to exchange its own paper money for oil anywhere on Earth, and that country is the U.S.A. Printing paper money and exchanging it for oil is a very valuable privilege; indeed, it is called the "exorbitant privilege" because it gives the owner of that currency unique (and from others' point of view, exorbitant) powers.

The one currency that is used by everyone around the world is called the "reserve currency." The U.S. dollar is the world's reserve currency. Oil is priced in dollars everywhere in the world.

How did the dollar become the world's reserve currency?

At one time, all currencies were backed by gold, meaning that each nation's central bank held gold in reserve that backed the value of its paper money. In a simple example, if a country had 1,000 ounces of gold, and it issued 1,000 paper bills of currency, each paper bill would be worth one ounce of gold, because the central bank promised to exchange the bill for an ounce of gold on demand.

The citizen holding the paper money would know it was always worth one ounce of gold.

If the nation's central bank issued 10,000 bills, then the value of each bill would be $1/10^{th}$ of an ounce of gold. Once again, the value was easily known by everyone.

The problem with this system is that in wartime, the costs of funding the war quickly exceed the limited amount of gold held in reserve, so governments start printing paper money to pay their war costs. The paper money quickly loses its value if the government prints too much. That causes runaway inflation and social instability, as savings lose value and trust in the paper money is lost.

In recessions, countries are tempted to devalue their currency to make their goods cheaper in other countries, boosting their exports. Other countries retaliate with trade restrictions, and trade is choked off, impoverishing every country that once prospered from trade.

As the end of World War II came into sight, the Allies established a monetary policy called the Bretton Woods system that established exchange rate stability. All currencies were pegged to the dollar, which was pegged to gold. Since the U.S. had vast reserves of gold, the dollar was in effect a substitute for gold.

But there was a serious problem with the system: the U.S., with its mighty industrial base intact, sold more goods to Europe and Japan than it bought from the war-ravaged nations. When a country exports more than it imports, it runs a trade surplus. (The opposite is called a trade deficit.) The problem with the U.S. surplus was that it sucked all the dollars out of Europe and Japan, leaving them insufficient dollars to develop industry and trade. Starved of dollars, the allies couldn't fund their reconstruction.

To solve this problem the U.S. loaned the allied governments millions of dollars; this was called the Marshall Plan. Once they had enough dollars to facilitate expansion and trade, Europe and Japan recovered quickly.

One way or another, the country issuing the reserve currency must distribute enough of its money into the global economy to grease trade and growth. This means the country issuing the reserve currency must run a large trade deficit when global trade is expanding rapidly.

This leads to some startling conclusions that many have difficulty accepting:

1. No nation whose domestic economy is based on exports and a trade surplus (i.e. they export more than they import) can issue the reserve currency. That eliminates the Chinese renminbi, the Japanese yen and the euro, as all these nations/trading blocs run trade surpluses or insignificant deficits. They simply can't deliver enough currency into the global economy for others to use.

2. Expanding global economic activity requires an expansion of reserves of the reserve currency, both for trade and as a foundation for each nation's own expansion of credit. Understood in this fashion, the huge increase in America's trade deficit (officially known as the "current account deficit") in the 2000s was essential to facilitate global expansion.

This means that to retain the exorbitant privilege of owning the world's reserve currency, the U.S. had to run massive trade deficits. As other countries need U.S. dollars for their own reserves and for expanding trade, the U.S. must import goods and export dollars for others to use. Regardless of what domestic policy makers may want, the U.S. has to run large trade deficits if it wants to retain the privileges of issuing the reserve currency.

This brings us to Triffin's Paradox, which is that the needs of the global trading community are different from the needs of domestic policy makers. This leads to conflicts of interest between short-term domestic policies and long-term international economic objectives. This dilemma was formulated by Belgian-American economist Robert Triffin in the 1960s, and it can be summarized in this way: the domestic economy wants a weak dollar so our exports are cheaper overseas, while the global economy needs the U.S. to maintain a strong dollar and run trade deficits so it has enough dollars to facilitate trade and provide foreign exchange reserves.

Global stability requires that trading nations hold large reserves of dollars. Here's why: the dollars stabilize the country's own currency. Each currency is priced in the foreign exchange (FX) market, and it can fluctuate due to political crises, devaluations, trade imbalances and other issues. While the world can never be sure of the value of a nation's currency in a crisis, everyone knows the value of the country's reserve of dollars; if it isn't quite "as good as gold," it is certainly a known quantity because the U.S. is a stable nation and 25% of the global economy.

Why am I explaining all this about the reserve currency and Triffin's Paradox? It is important for all Americans to understand that there is an enormous benefit to being the one nation that can print money and exchange it for goods and services anywhere on Earth. But like all great privileges, it comes with responsibilities, and our responsibility is to supply the global economy with the dollars needed for reserves and trade. That means we cannot run trade surpluses, nor can we endlessly depreciate our dollar.

Our wealth and prosperity have many foundations, but owning and issuing the world's reserve currency is an almost incalculable advantage.

This brings us to globalization. Many feel that globalization has been bad for America, and that trade deficits are also bad for America. We need to separate trade policies from globalization; every nation has the right to protect itself from exploitation and to manage its trade. But globalization via the reserve currency is the international foundation of American privilege and power, and we would be foolish to squander that because we don't understand Triffin's Paradox.

Globalization does not mean meddling in others' affairs; it means maintaining a stable framework for voluntary "win-win" trade. The U.S. and other nations have grown prosperous from trade and a flexible, global foreign exchange system. I mentioned earlier the difference between China and India and the West in the 16th century; China and India clung to the rigid notion of gold and silver as the one true form of wealth, and they shriveled as their capital lay dormant in treasure houses and trade withered. Meanwhile the West invested its capital in industry, trade and capital markets, and it rapidly outran the older, wealthier, more advanced nations that had stagnated with vaults of gold and silver and meager trade.

The China of the Tang Dynasty (700 to 900 A.D.) was wealthy and powerful precisely because goods flowed freely over its stable land and sea routes, and its currency and goods were accepted throughout the trading world. We can all learn from its example.

The Diminishing Returns of Centralization

For the past two centuries, the economies and political systems of the West have been increasing centralization. To reap greater efficiencies and profits, small companies were relentlessly consolidated into large global corporations and governments centralized power.

At the turn of the 20th century, the only institution of the Federal government most people interacted with was the Post Office. The Armed Forces were limited, Federal agencies were small, there was no income tax and very few people ever dealt with Federal laws or the court system. Now over 50% of the population gets a check or benefit from the Federal government, and it dominates and controls every aspect of our lives.

In the private sector, the ideal centralization is complete ownership of a market, what we call a monopoly. Why is a monopoly so ideal for the owners? Once competition has been eliminated, you can charge whatever you want and reap enormous profits at basically zero risk.

The next best model is a cartel, a small handful of large corporations that divvy up the market and fix prices so everyone makes huge profits.

There were no laws against buying up or squeezing competitors, and so it was legal to assemble a monopoly or cartel. Eventually J.D. Rockefeller created a vast monopoly for distributing oil in the U.S. Since oil is the lifeblood of an industrial economy, this was recognized as being negative for the economy and society, and monopolies were broken up and outlawed.

Nonetheless this same business model of centralization is with us today: the five "too big to fail" banks that have been saved by Federal Reserve intervention each became "too big to fail" by consolidating and buying up dozens of smaller banks. The "too big to fail" banks are a cartel that became so powerful it could demand the government pony up $16 trillion to protect it from collapse.

You see what happens when centralization reaches the level of total control: it diverts the surplus of the productive citizenry to the unproductive few and becomes a vested interest that is wealthy enough to buy political protection from competition.

What was touted as being more efficient—centralization—becomes terribly inefficient as the quality of the goods and services decline in monopoly while the price goes up. Why bother improving quality or service if customers have no choice?

Capitalism only works when competition is present and the inefficient and corrupt are replaced by more efficient models, a process known as "creative destruction." Once competition and creative destruction have been eliminated, capitalism fails and what's left is monopoly, dictatorship or feudalism.

Government has no competition. It has a monopoly on coercion, taxation, investigation and a host of other powers. When a monopoly of political power (the government) partners with a monopoly of financial power (banks and global corporations), the result is crony capitalism: a neofeudalism that is "capitalist" in name only because competition and creative destruction have both been eliminated.

With the advent of the Internet and new fabrication and service technologies, decentralized businesses and governments can provide faster, better and cheaper goods and services than monopolies and cartels. The model of ever-greater centralization no longer yields a higher return; rather, it is now sapping the lifeblood from productive sectors of the society and destroying widespread prosperity and democracy.

There are some fabrication facilities that still benefit from centralized production, for example, semiconductor computer processors, because the process is so complex that it can only be done in large facilities. But the model that centralization delivers more value is failing in industry after industry, including the government sector. Centralization doesn't mean efficiency so much as elimination of competition and the transfer of wealth from the productive to the unproductive but politically powerful.

The Internet is powerful because it is distributed, decentralized and transparent—everything that monopolies, cartels and centralized government are not.

Monopoly, cartels and government are centralized concentrations power and wealth. The Internet is disruptive precisely because it is more efficient, faster and cheaper than these centralized skimming operations that gain their power from centralization and lack of transparency.

As noted earlier, centralization inevitably leads to collapse of the economy and society as the unproductive centralized entity increasingly poaches off the remaining productive sectors to fund its inefficiencies, eventually bleeding them dry. The entire Status Quo then collapses.

This is the essential dynamic behind the stagnation of all centralized economies, be they crony-capitalist, socialist or Communist. Beneath the surface label they are identical.

Summary

Demographics, decline of paid work, diminishing returns, globalization, centralization, erosion of civil liberties, the end of cheap energy and the cultural contradictions of capitalism will not go away even if we resolve our dysfunctional financial and political systems. They will require structural changes in our economy, government, society and culture.

Section Four:
Prosperity and Happiness

The Declaration of Independence famously grouped life, liberty and the pursuit of happiness as inalienable rights. The freedom to better oneself and one's life is core to the American Dream, and the general assumption is that prosperity and wealth increase happiness. The pursuit of happiness has become the pursuit of prosperity and wealth.

That physical comfort and security grease the skids of happiness are self-evident; living a hand-to-mouth existence in a cardboard box is not as conducive to human happiness as having a comfortable home and secure income.

But it is equally self-evident that a secure dwelling and income do not guarantee happiness; rather, they provide the foundation for the much more elusive qualities of happiness. We can make the same distinction between the civil liberties that underpin the pursuit of happiness and the actual pursuit of happiness. The first is a political system devoted to safeguarding liberty; the second is a messy, dynamic process that continues through all of life.

If prosperity and wealth generate greater happiness, we might expect to find prosperous people are generally happy; it is not surprising that more prosperous nations report higher degrees of satisfaction and happiness than nations mired in poverty.

America has great material wealth, but is happiness as abundant as wealth? If not, why not?

Numerous psychologists have made a career of studying happiness, and as with all social sciences, the field is wide open to cherry-picking data to support a prepackaged view. But data from studies of happiness is suspect for the usual reasons: people tend to report what they sense is expected of them; they tend to make themselves appear more successful (i.e. "happier") than they really are, and the results can be skewed by the questions and procedures of the study.

The vast majority of such studies are conducted within a specific mindset: happiness is an individual issue: fundamentally, "it's all in your head" and "the system enables happiness, so unhappiness is your fault alone."

The "fix" for unhappiness in this paradigm is a carefully apolitical network of pressure relief valves: counseling, therapy, motivational speakers, and so on, all focused on "fixing" the flaws within individuals that are assumed to be the exclusive cause of their unhappiness.

As a result of my work on *Resistance, Revolution, Liberation: A Model for Positive Change*, I now question the assumption that our happiness is disconnected from the society and economy we live in. What if unhappiness is not just an individual failure but the consequence of a deeply distorted society? If this is the case, prosperity in the sense of material wealth cannot possibly yield anything but the fleeting pleasure of consumption.

"Life, liberty and the pursuit of happiness" have been distilled into a sociopathology of consumption and unrealistic expectations of "prosperity" that do not lead to either happiness or well-being.

A Critique of Happiness

Though we think of happiness as a private pursuit, in aggregate the pursuit of happiness becomes what we might call a public happiness. As author Garry Wills observed, public happiness is the test and justification of any government. If individual happiness is made difficult by the State, then that State must be judged a failure.

Public happiness is not just the aggregation of individual happiness; it is a reflection of the social and political order's success in enabling the common good, one expression of which is the potential for individual fulfillment.

In our carefully cultivated atmosphere of individuality, it is heresy to question the assumption that individual fulfillment is apolitical. This Status Quo breaks the causal connection between private alienation and the political order so the atomized individual doesn't connect his own unhappiness with the sociopathologies of the consumerist-State social order.

The isolated "consumer" doesn't look at the social order as a potential contributor to his unhappiness but instead looks to religion, psychotherapy or medications as private solutions to the sociopathology he inhabits.

The spiritual and psychological traditions of religion and psychotherapy serve as coping mechanisms for individuals as they navigate the many challenges of human existence; intended to provide insight and solace for the voyage through life, these traditions were not designed to analyze pathological social orders. They are apolitical because they address problems from the point of view of faith and inner understanding.

That we have no field exclusively devoted to understanding systemic sociopathologies is not surprising once we understand the politics of self-interest. How many mortals would place their own prosperity at risk by undermining the intellectual foundations of the Status Quo to which they belong? History suggests that few individuals have the courage to risk status and wealth by undermining the social order that bestows their perquisites.

Social orders that excel in creating and distributing what I term *social defeat* will necessarily be populated with unhappy, depressed, anxious and frustrated people, regardless of the material prosperity they possess.

In my lexicon, social defeat is a spectrum of anxiety, insecurity, chronic stress, powerlessness and fear of declining social status.

One aspect of social defeat is the emptiness we experience when prosperity does not deliver the promised sense of fulfillment. Here is one example. A recent sociological study compared wealthy Hong Kong residents' sense of contentment with those of the immigrant maids who served the moneyed Elites. The study found the maids were much happier than their wealthy masters, who were often suicidal and depressed. The maids, on the other hand, had a trustworthy group— other maids they met on their one day off—and the coherent purpose provided by their support of their families back home.

The "American Dream" (as well as the "Chinese Dream") presumes the opposite would be true, and this explains why reaching material abundance is not the promised fount of fulfillment: it fails to recognize the other necessary conditions of human happiness. It is a monoculture of the spirit, as brittle and prone to collapse as any other monoculture.

Sociopathology and Stress

The physiology of stress illuminates many of the dynamics we see manifesting in the poor mental and physical health of the American populace and in their passivity in the political and financial realms.

There is a growing body of evidence that unremitting stress has a number of subtle and destructive consequences to both mental and physical health. In addition to the common-sense connection between chronic stress and hypertension, evidence is mounting that obesity and other so-called "lifestyle" diseases are causally linked to stress-related conditions such as inadequate sleep and chronic inflammation.

Western medicine traditionally divides physical and mental health, but it is self-evident (as Eastern traditions have long held) that the mind and body are one. The physical consequences of mental stress make this abundantly clear, as the powerful hormones that we experience as "mental stress" erode the immune system's responsiveness.

Behaviorally, stress fuels addictive disorders by breaking down the self-control that inhibits destructive bingeing, impulse buying, unsafe sex and drug/alcohol abuse.

The consequences of chronic stress are multiplied by our reliance (or perhaps more accurately, our addiction) to digital media and communication. Clinically, these manifestations have recently been termed Attention Deficit Trait or ADT, a broader, more inclusive term than the more familiar Attention Deficit Disorder.

ADT manifests as distractibility, inner frenzy, impatience and difficulty in setting priorities, time management and making informed decisions. As these loop into positive feedback, previously competent people become harried underachievers who berate themselves for their inexplicable loss of competence.

ADT, unlike post-traumatic stress disorders triggered by a single event, arises not from a single crisis but from a chain of events that in less stressful times would be considered "a bad week" but in chronic stress are experienced as an unending series of emergencies. The response—to try harder to keep up and successfully manage the crises—only increases the stress load and sense of failure as the ability to rationally analyze and pursue plans degrades with each perceived emergency. Making matters worse, the conventional American "solution" to being overwhelmed is to avoid expressing these difficulties lest this be interpreted as complaining.

This is the consequence of chronic stress (burnout) being normalized: an accurate description of the condition is dismissed as whining and the truth-teller is instructed to keep his head down and his nose to the grindstone.

With the rational mind and self-control centers suppressed, we are prone to "zombie-like" passivity, in effect "sleepwalking" though life. This dynamic may help explain Americans' remarkable political passivity as their civil liberties are curtailed and their financial insecurity increases.

The stresses created by these pathologies are not abstract; rather, they lead to the self-destructive behaviors that are now ubiquitous in America: impulsiveness, addiction, abuse of drugs and alcohol (often attempts to self-medicate social defeat), obesity, impoverished sense of self, low level of fitness and vitality, inability to concentrate or complete coherently organized tasks, high levels of distraction and passivity and a loss of resilience and self-reliance.

This is not to say that all disorders arise solely from pathological social orders; a percentage of the human population is genetically vulnerable to mental disorders, and life itself is filled with challenges and unwelcome surprises that create stress. The question being explored here is: since it is self-evident that the financial and political order we inhabit influences our mental and physical well-being, what are the long-term consequences to individuals living in a sociopathological system of financial neofeudalism, an autocratic, expansive Central State that enforces extremes of wealth and power and an unparalleled corporate marketing/media propaganda machine?

Anyone who claims these pathologies have negligible effect on individuals' well-being is either in denial or is a well-paid shill for the Status Quo.

The net effect of chronic stress is the ability to implement coherently organized positive plans—the foundation of fulfillment—is severely impaired. This explains why happiness is so difficult to understand and why it is even more difficult to sustainably pursue in a pathological system that disrupts our capacity for rational analysis, self-control and coherent action.

Consumerism, Happiness and Power

The notion that increased consumption leads to increased happiness is self-evidently false, yet consumption remains the focus of our economy and society. The appeal of consumption is understandable once we grasp that it is the only empowering act in a neofeudal society where we are essentially powerless.

In the mindset of the consumerist economy, purchasing something feels empowering because the act of consuming is experienced as renewing our sense of identity and social status. But since that identity is inauthentic, the sense of euphoric renewal is short-lived, and soon defaults to the base state of insecurity.

Since the consumer is only empowered by buying and displaying status signifiers, the balance of their lives is experienced as powerless: that is, a chronic state of social defeat.

In the act of consuming, the only feature that continues on after the initial euphoria fades is the debt taken on to make the purchase.

In Part II, we consider the foundations of a sustainable pursuit of happiness outside the sociopathological Status Quo.

If material prosperity is necessary but insufficient, and our social and financial order is sociopathological, what does an authentic pursuit of happiness entail?

For answers, we can survey recent research into human happiness, and consider "powering down" participation in a deranging social and financial order.

Happiness and Power

The primacy of power in human society is omnipresent. Humans scramble for power in all its forms to improve social status and the odds of mating, living a long life and acquiring comforts. What is remarkable about the current American social order is the powerlessness of the vast majority of people who have "bought into" the Status Quo.

When the public vehemently disapproves of a policy, such as bailing out the "too big to fail" banks, they are routinely ignored, and for good reason: they keep re-electing incumbents. Most have little control over their employment status, workflow or income, and most devote the majority of their productive effort servicing private debt and paying taxes that service public debt.

The one "power" they are encouraged to flex is the momentary empowerment offered by purchasing something, i.e. consuming. The corporate marketing machine glorifies acquisition as not just empowering but as the renewal of identity and the staking of a claim to higher social status—everything that is otherwise out of the control of the average person.

The dominant social control myth of our consumerist Status Quo is that wealth is power because you can buy more things with it. But the power of consumption is one-dimensional and therefore illusory. The only meaningful power is not what you can buy (a good, service or experience) but what you control: your health, choice of work, income, surroundings, level of risk and your circle of colleagues and friends.

The "wealthy" who own an abundance of things but who are trapped in debt are not powerful. Their choices in life are limited by the need to service the debt, and their pursuit of happiness is equally constrained.

The kind of wealth that enriches the pursuit of happiness is control over the meaningful aspects of life. It is no coincidence that studies of workplace stress have found that those jobs in which the worker has almost no control over their work or surroundings generate far more stress than jobs that allow the worker some autonomy and control.

Financial and material wealth beyond the basics of creature comfort is only meaningful if it "buys" autonomy and choice.

We all want power over our own lives. Once we free ourselves from social control myths, we find that becoming powerful and "wealthy" in terms of control does not require a financial fortune. It does however require sustained effort and a coherent long-term plan.

Breaking Free of Debt and Consumerism

Another key social control myth is that debt-servitude, social defeat and a sense of failure are either "all in your head" or the result of your own flaws. But sociopathology exists both in the mind of those who have internalized the social control myth and in the real world; the financialized, debt-dependent economy is not a figment of imagination that we can will away or transform with an attitude adjustment. Debt-serfdom is the dominant mode of the real world.

An abundance of money is not the same as financial independence. Financial independence means liberation from debt and dependence on debt-based payments from the Central State. Such independence is less a function of great wealth and more a function of self-reliance, resilience and the attainment of the other conditions of fulfillment and happiness: work you care about, people you care about and who care about you, and opportunities to positively renew identity and social standing in cooperative settings. Such non-market settings enable the cultivation of what we call social capital.

The myth that the acquisition of things offers power, social status and identity is ceaselessly promoted by corporate marketing and the media. Anyone who steps away from the myth's spotlight is in danger of being viewed as a "failure," as the Status Quo vigorously defends its myths by showering dissenters with social defeat. Those who decide to "power down" their debt, income and accompanying social status signifiers may find themselves subjected to social ostracism by conventional colleagues and the protests of household members who are still in the grip of the consumerist mythologies.

Want, Need and Well-Being

Though the difference between a want and a need is self-explanatory, recent research has illuminated their connection to happiness.

In terms of our "hard-wiring," the gratification of both need and want trigger a reward system in our "hedonic" neural circuitry. We seem to enjoy what we "want" more than what we "like." (No wonder consumerism is such an easy sell.)

A "need" can veer off into an addiction, where the satisfaction of the need does not stimulate sensations of pleasure (i.e. the experience of happiness). Gratifying a want or desire, on the other hand, offers pleasure up to the point of satiation, what might be called "the chocolate chip cookie" phenomenon where the first cookie triggers enjoyment but the satisfaction gained from consuming additional cookies diminishes to the point of discomfort.

Aristotle reckoned that happiness consisted of *hedonia* (pleasure) and *eudaimonia* (a sense of meaning). Consumerist marketing appeals to the innate pleasure in meeting a want or need (and arguably, stimulates addiction to shopping and debt) but it fails to address our need for meaning. The consumerist myth attempts to supply "meaning" in the guise of social status, but the store-bought identity is devoid of meaning.

Expectation, Narrative and Challenge

One reason that higher-income groups tend to be less happy than their lower-income peers is the level of expectation: those who have unrealistically high expectations of themselves and life tend to be disappointed and depressed by their perceived failure. This suggests that one key to the successful pursuit of happiness is realistic expectations of oneself, others and life.

Once again we can trace the unhappiness of unmet expectations to consumerist marketing that elevates the standards of "success" to such absurd heights that only a few people can reach the desired mountaintop: who is attractive enough, successful enough, credentialed enough, thin enough and wealthy enough to qualify? Impossibly high expectations lead to unhappiness and social defeat, even in the accomplished. If a society excels in distributing social defeat but is parsimonious with positive social standing, then the majority of its citizens will be alienated, anxious, depressed and prone to drug abuse and despair.

Anecdotal evidence suggests that those people with a positive personal narrative are happier than those with a negative narrative or "story of my life." In other words, the way we frame our experience of obstacles, failures, goals, disappointments and successes informs the *eudaimonia* aspect of our well-being.

Thus those people who internalize "powering down" consumerist definitions of happiness as a positive plan to improve their well-being that requires long years of hard work and sacrifice will be happier than those who view a lower standard of consumption as a social and financial defeat.

Clearly, having a supportive circle of like-minded family, friends and colleagues makes it much easier to "power down" a consumer-based life and identity. I personally long for the inevitable counter-revolution that will make shunning consumerist excess "cool."

Much has been written about the "purpose-driven life," one way of describing our innate need for meaning (*eudaimonia*). Less has been written about the role of challenges, obstacles and failure in creating the "meaning" component of happiness. Anecdotally, we can observe that those who are given things without any effort do not value what they were given, and indeed, are prone to a corrosive resentment and self-absorption. Happiness does not flow from being given money and possessions with no strings attached but from perseverance in the face of hardship, obstacles, challenges and failures.

Resilience is a key feature of self-reliance, and the learned ability to pick oneself up after a failure and press on is a key attribute of resilience. The smallest personal victory is immensely more fulfilling than the unearned entitlement, and so resilience and self-reliance are not just useful survival traits, they are building blocks of happiness.

Foundations of Happiness

What are the foundations of happiness and fulfillment? Let's start with these basics:

- A secure standing in a stable, trustworthy group
- An internally coherent worldview that makes sense of one's experiences
- Meaningful ways to contribute, earn the essentials of life and fashion a positive identity
- Opportunities for expression, movement, marriage, association, worship and enterprise
- A positive personal narrative
- Realistic expectations

- Long-term, coherent plans to lower dependency on pathological, failed systems and increase control of work, surroundings, financial and social capital and support networks
- Sustainable health and a healthy lifestyle

This list runs counter to the assumptions underpinning most developed world economies, where having an abundance of money ("wealth") is seen as the one essential key to happiness and fulfillment.

No wonder so many who achieve this coveted state of financial abundance find instead dissatisfaction, alienation and emptiness. The reason is simple: money can buy creature comforts, but it does not provide a coherent worldview, purpose, a trustworthy group or a meaningful identity. It provides superficial placeholders for these needs, but this substitution only creates an equally hollow facsimile of fulfillment.

We have four ways to counter the destructive effects of sociopathologically generated stress:

1) Develop positive physical and mental responses to stress via discipline and practice (for example, yoga, martial arts, meditation/prayer, walking, bicycling, etc.)

2) Withdraw from sociopathological influences such as the mainstream media "news"

3) Pursue a healthy, non-pathological "reset" system to replace the current Status Quo when it implodes in financial insolvency and political instability

4) Remain focused on coherently organized plans. The simpler and more positive the plan, the more likely it is we can stay focused on it in increasingly stressful circumstances.

Support Sustainable Alternatives

To the degree that we "vote" not just in elections but with every purchase and choice we make, we can support or opt out (i.e. refuse to participate) of a great many Status Quo systems such as debt. Since our complicity or resistance to systems is part of our purpose and meaning, identifying the systems we will support is at least tangentially related to our happiness and well-being. Do we support the Status Quo, or do we support sustainable alternatives that add to the common good?

There is so much more that could be said about happiness, and I hope you understand that I have only scratched the surface. If there is "one last thing" to note, it is the connection between our individual happiness and the happiness of the community and society. As noted above, public happiness is not just the aggregation of individual happiness; it is a reflection of the financial and political order's success in enabling the common good. We are each part of that common good.

Summary

The models that have fueled our current prosperity—financialization, centralization, excessive leverage and debt, speculative bubbles, expansion of the Central State, Federal Reserve manipulation, cheap oil—are no longer working; the return on these models has diminished to zero. In the span of only four years, 2009 to 2012, we have borrowed and squandered $6 trillion, printed another $2 trillion and propped up the banking sector with $16 trillion in guarantees, yet the economy is stagnant and income disparity continues to widen.

Rather than bemoan the decline of phantom prosperity based on bubbles, fraud and debt, we can look at bettering our lives by moving beyond consumption as the sole yardstick of wealth and happiness.

Section Five:
Understanding Systems

Much of what we think is permanent is crumbling because the basic system no longer works; the returns on the borrowed money that keeps the system going are diminishing to zero. We're running faster every year, so to speak, just to maintain our current position. Once the wheel of debt spins a bit faster, we'll quickly lose ground and the system will collapse.

Humanity has learned a great deal about the way systems work in the past 50 years, but virtually none of this knowledge has seeped into government or the crony-capitalist cartel system. As we have seen, these are still based on centralization and ever-increasing concentrations of wealth and power—the very causes of instability and collapse.

The entrenched vested interests will never allow the system to decentralize because that would deprive them of their extractive premiums.

As noted previously, the monopoly of government and the cartels it protects are draining the lifeblood from the few remaining productive sectors. This vast transfer of surplus from the productive to the unproductive is not enough, so the Central State must borrow trillions of dollars every year. Add the inefficiency, fraud, corruption and friction of the present system to rising interest payments and you have a surefire recipe for collapse.

Since the Status Quo can't be fixed, we must look beyond failed models to new models of sustainable prosperity. To really understand the new models, we first need to understand something about the way systems work.

Systems that look very different on the surface actually share basic characteristics. Broadly speaking, quantifying these shared traits is the task of systems analysis.

Systems Have a "Mind" of their Own

There are shelves of books on system dynamics, but we're going to summarize the key attributes of systems in a few pages.

The primary fantasy of central planning, and indeed, centralization, is that everything in a complex system can be controlled, either directly or indirectly with manipulation or slight-of-hand. That's not the way systems work.

Complex systems cannot be controlled, no matter how complex the controls may be, for reasons we'll cover below.

What makes a system complex? There are several factors. One is the total number of participants in the system, another is the number of "nodes" that can influence the system and the third is the number of connections between nodes.

The brain is almost unimaginably complex because billions of "nodes" (neurons) are interconnected to many other nodes. We call these connections feedback loops, as the signals traveling between nodes influence future signals and all the other nodes receiving and sending signals.

In a very real way, any large complex system is actually a system of systems. Our economy and society are systems made up of thousands of other systems. Together, all these systems connect millions of participants and billions of transactions and signals.

The complex system we all can observe in action is the ecosystem around us. When central planning attempts to "make" the ecosystem work in a certain way, the system responds with unforeseen consequences. For example, by eliminating birds because they eat some of their grain crop, farmers trigger an insect infestation that destroys their entire crop. The birds kept the insects under control and so when you eliminate the birds, the insect population explodes.

Systems are like rubber bands: if you stretch them one way to suit your purposes, eventually they "snap back."

The joke in this subtitle is that complex (nonlinear) systems do not have a "mind" at all. They have parameters and feedback loops of inputs and outputs. These few elements interact in dynamic and unpredictable ways on their own, without central control.

Here's the difference between linear and complex systems. Linear systems lend themselves to causal chains like dominoes (A causes B which causes C) or probability (the odds of drawing two aces in a game of Blackjack) that can be calibrated with a high degree of accuracy.

Complex systems exhibit fractal or chaotic characteristics that make them prone to disruption by seemingly small events. System stability requires constant variation and fluctuations and a free flow of information and feedback. If "undesirable" fluctuations and feedback are restricted, the system loses stability and becomes increasingly prone to instability and collapse.

In financial terms, risk and volatility are the constantly shifting variations that give the system stability. In political terms, dissent provides variation. Author Nassim Taleb has explained that "variation is information:" starve the system of variation and you starve it of the information flow it needs to remain stable.

Taleb explained this dynamic in the June 2011 issue of *Foreign Affairs* magazine: "Complex systems that have artificially suppressed volatility become extremely fragile, while at the same time exhibiting no visible risks."

When volatility and dissent are suppressed by central authorities, the variations that inform an open market and democracy are lost. Once variations are lost, both the free market and democracy are destabilized and become prone to unpredictable collapse.

Central planning attempts to engineer a false stability by suppressing "undesirable" volatility have created an intrinsically fragile system that is doomed to crises of ever greater amplitude even as the periods of calm between crises shrink from years to months.

This kind of imposed stability breeds complacency which then breeds risk-taking which then leads to collapse. (Remember our "casino" example.)

Recall that risk is like water in a closed system: it can never be squeezed into nothingness. When central authorities declare risk has been banished, it becomes inevitable that the suppressed risk will burst out in some part of the financial system that was viewed as "safe and stable," for example, home mortgages.

This is how financial events that are widely viewed by conventional economists and government officials as "impossible" can occur with increasing frequency.

One model for this type of apparent stability that is destabilized by unpredictable events is stick/slip destabilization. In "sticky" systems, pressure builds up that is invisible to those looking at an apparently stable surface. But at some impossible-to-predict moment, the built-up pressure within completely disrupts the system, and it "slips" into a new configuration.

This kind of unpredictable collapse is nonlinear, meaning that it unfolds very rapidly, rather like an avalanche. The system is vulnerable, but on the surface all looks stable. Some small event unleashes the built-up instability and the avalanche crashes down.

Another way of understanding this is that unsustainable, unaffordable systems break down and reorganize at a level that is affordable. Since complexity is costly, these systems will restabilize at a level that is much simpler as well as much cheaper.

We Don't Choose an Alternative System: Whatever Is Faster, Better and Cheaper Wins

When we talk about an alternative to the failing Status Quo system, we need to understand that we don't get to choose an alternative system. That's not the way systems work: whatever is faster, better, cheaper and sustainable will replace what is inefficient, costly and unsustainable. If we choose a costly, inefficient, fraud-riddle system, it will soon collapse and be replaced by whatever is sustainable and affordable.

As we noted above, systems are networks of interconnected nodes that exchange signals (feedback). Any node that influences many other nodes is a leverage point: changes in that one node act as leverage on all the nodes it's connected to. The more nodes and signals there are, the more information the system can process and the more adaptable it becomes.

The Internet has vastly increased the number of leverage points, nodes and signals in the global network of information, ideas, goods and services, and so adaptation and evolution has been speeded up.

Think about inventions as an example. As technology became more expensive and complex, the number of institutions that could afford research and development shrank. In the early 1900s, the Wright Brothers developed an airplane in their bicycle shop; by the 1950s, only a handful of large corporations could afford to develop new aircraft.

The number of leverage-point nodes of innovation actually declined.

Compare that to the present-day Internet, where a handful of young people working in a garage or dorm room can launch entire industries and innovations that spread around the world in a matter of months. The number of potentially influential (leverage point) nodes has expanded into the tens of millions, and the cost of innovation in many industries has declined dramatically.

The more nodes there are that can create and distribute innovation, the more innovations will be introduced, and the faster change will evolve.

So what we're talking about here is not choosing a system in the way we choose a political constitution; we're trying to understand that systems made up of millions of other systems will evolve on their own as participants learn about alternatives and make decisions based on feedback and innovations.

Whatever is faster, better, cheaper and sustainable will win as participants choose what works better for them. We may want centralized, costly systems dependent on expanding debt to endure, but they will not survive because they are unaffordable. What will replace them is whatever is faster, better, cheaper and sustainable.

Creative Destruction and Faster, Better, Cheaper

Economist Joseph Schumpeter described how capitalism's key function is "creative destruction": new technologies, processes and ideas dismantle and replace less efficient models. In the industrial economy, the number of leverage points ("network nodes") capable of developing and launching new technology and ideas was limited to a handful of corporations and government agencies because the expense and *information asymmetry* was so great.

As information asymmetry fades, many of the jobs that were once the exclusive domain of government can be done faster, better and cheaper by fast-adapting enterprises and voluntary communities.

Centralized government is based on the model of slowly developing regulations that detail how complex systems should work. The more complex the system, the more complex the laws and regulations the government creates to oversee the system.

Consider the Glass-Steagall Act of 1933 that was 37 pages long, and the 2,319-page "Dodd-Frank Wall Street Reform and Consumer Protection Act" that was passed after the 2008 global financial crisis.

Meanwhile, the banking sector that is supposed to be controlled by this immensely complex law has already moved beyond the reach of the law or bought political favors to protect its interests. As noted earlier, the "revolving door" allows those who crafted the law to go to work for the banks being regulated, and for lobbyists representing the banks to write key sections of the new law.

Once again, the public has effectively zero knowledge and insiders enjoy information asymmetry which they use to their advantage.

Any process that can be corrupted by bribes, self-serving political intervention and information asymmetry is open to abuse of power, and so its regulatory function is undermined by the very process of its creation.

Central government is simply too expensive, too complex and too corruptible to manage a complex economy that is rapidly adapting to the pressures of faster, better, c heaper. The information asymmetry the government tries to maintain ends up protecting the very forces of monopoly and corruption that are driving the economy over the cliff.

Natural Selection: How Systems Adapt and Evolve

Natural selection is simply the process of whatever is advantageous spreading through the group. In Nature, genetic variations (recall that variation is information and necessary for stability) offer experimental advantages to organisms. Some are so marginal that they don't offer much advantage to the possessor of the new trait, and so the variation disappears from the gene pool. Those few that offer distinct advantages eventually spread throughout the gene pool.

Organisms are living systems, as are ecosystems. Enterprises, neighborhoods and cities are all systems as well. Natural selection—the generation of variation to gain advantageous adaptations—is how systems evolve. This is true not just of organisms but of enterprises, cities and nations. Those systems which fail to generate variation (information) cannot generate advantageous adaptations and thus they cannot evolve. As the world changes, stagnant systems cannot compete with evolving systems so they decline and vanish.

Centralized systems are prone to suppressing variation as threatening; decentralized systems by their very nature generate ample variation. This is the primary reason why centralized systems are doomed to fail: they lack the essentials needed to adapt and evolve. Their core nature is to suppress transparency, variation and dissent as threats to the vested interests that benefit from centralization.

This is why our Status Quo is increasingly vulnerable to nonlinear destabilization and collapse.

We all understand why companies that fail to evolve and adapt end up going bankrupt: they lost touch with their customers, didn't generate advantageous adaptations and were superseded by companies with faster, better, cheaper products and services.

The same is true of local government: cities, counties and states. Local governments controlled by self-serving vested interests cannot adapt, as any change would threaten the vested interests that are reaping extractive premiums. This transfer from the productive to the unproductive eventually motivates the productive residents to move away to less feudal locales. That leaves the vested interests without "cash cows" to milk, and the local Status Quo collapses under its own unproductive weight.

Local government is also a system, and if it is extractive, inefficient, sclerotic and ruled by feudal vested interests (public unions, corporate cartels, etc.) then it cannot adapt or evolve. Rather than welcome the variation required for stability, it suppresses dissent and transparency as threats to the Powers That Be. That unwillingness to adapt and evolve dooms the local government to collapse.

This leads us to an important conclusion: if the local governments of state, county and city are feudal, extractive, opaque and protect vested interests, they will drain the lifeblood from the productive to support their vested interests. It is impossible to prosper in such feudal conditions, and so it is necessary for the productive to move to locales that welcome variation, transparency and a willingness to adapt and evolve: these are the building blocks of stability and prosperity. This requires a decentralized government structure that is not beholden to self-serving vested interests.

Local governments without these traits will inevitably go bankrupt. The same is also true of enterprises and national governments.

Natural selection works both ways: we can either select for variation, experimentation, transparency and advantageous adaptation or we can select for decline and collapse.

How Systems Collapse

Ultimately, the foundation of all financial systems and institutions is the trust and confidence of participants. Trust is nonlinear, meaning that faith in institutions erodes slowly until it reaches a "tipping point" where some event triggers a loss of confidence that cascades into a total collapse of the system.

Currencies collapse in this way, bank runs start this way, and people abandon institutions this way. As with our avalanche example, things look stable on the surface until the avalanche suddenly thunders down the mountain. That's how nonlinear systems collapse.

Why do systems fail? We can identify a few key dynamics:

1. Malinvestment: resources and surpluses are not infinite. We can print money in unlimited quantities but you can't print oil, iron ore, grain, etc. Once the available resources have been squandered, there aren't enough left to maintain the system.

When resources are devoted to projects with diminishing returns, those resources are unavailable for critical maintenance and investment in the future—the foundation of productivity and prosperity. Every expenditure has an opportunity cost that is not on the price tag: what other investment will now go begging because the money has been spent propping up the Status Quo?

The central fantasy of America is "no limits": there is always enough money for everything we want. Money may be plentiful but resources are not. Once the resources are no longer available to sustain a high-cost complex structure, it erodes and collapses.

2. Complex interlocking systems: when the weakest link in an interlocking system fails, that failure cascades into all the connected subsystems, collapsing the entire system.

Long supply chains of sole-source suppliers illustrate this. When a key factory goes down, the entire supply chain is disrupted. These systems are not fault-tolerant: the failure of any critical part quickly brings the whole system to its knees.

Leverage and debt are key components in the "supply chain" of our economy. Reduce them and the system quickly destabilizes.

3. Complexity itself leads to destabilization, as interlocking complex systems overwhelm our ability to understand how failures are triggered and how they cascade through hyper-complex systems. Complexity has costs and risks that are not apparent during times of stability.

4. Risk cannot be eliminated, it can only be transferred. Suppressed risk flows to parts of the system that are considered "safe." For example, the expansion of risky derivatives and leverage flowed to the "safe" mortgage market. The failure of subprime mortgages then spread, triggering the global financial system crisis.

5. Hubris and complacency. The waning days of Imperial Rome were characterized by complacent confidence: the general attitude was "we've gotten through worse spots than this in our long glorious history," as if invoking past triumphs over adversity could substitute for actual hard-choice policies and living within their dwindling means.

The same magical-thinking belief in the permanence of the Savior State characterizes the American mindset: "we'll get through this somehow" is no substitute for realistic assessments and radical reorganization.

The Highway System in 1910 and the Internet in 1980

Readers often express frustration that I do not provide specific details on these future sustainable systems. I understand their frustration, as we all prefer a well-defined "roadmap" with simple instructions. For example, many analysts recommend buying gold as the "solution" to riding out the instability ahead. That is admirably easy to understand and simple to follow, but buying gold won't create sustainable systems.

I wish I could provide details about future systems, but I cannot, for the reason that the systems in question are like the highway system in 1910 and the Internet in 1980: the barest bones are visible but the real development lies ahead. Readers wanting "specifics" are like people asking for directions to interstate highway on-ramps in 1910—they don't even exist in the imagination, much less the real world.

The Internet existed in 1980 in rudimentary form, but if you'd asked for "specifics" about how to design your web page you would have drawn blank stares: the web browser was still 15 years in the future.

All I can do is sketch out the bare bones of sustainable systems. The infrastructure exists in a very preliminary fashion, sometimes in the real world, sometimes only in the imagination. The real work of making new systems accessible to all lies ahead.

Principles, Not Operating Instructions

One feature of complex systems is that they develop in unpredictable ways. As a result, complex systems are best understood with principles rather than detailed instructions. In this, they are like "real life." In daily life, we don't try to follow 2,000 pages of detailed instructions; since life is dynamic and unpredictable, detailed instructions would quickly prove cumbersome or even misleading.

Instead, we follow principles of conduct, response and organization. For example, we might use the OODA loop (observe, orient, decide, and act) developed by Colonel John Boyd (USAF). What we observe, how we orient ourselves, what we decide and how we act are not detailed, as life is too complex to offer instructions for every circumstance. Instead, we use principles that can be usefully applied to a variety of situations.

The political Status Quo has attempted to write detailed operating instructions for the five "too big to fail" banks, passing a law with over 2,300 pages of statutes that require hundreds of additional pages of regulations and reports.

The only practical system reverses the numbers: the five "too big to fail" banks should be broken up into 2,300 smaller banks that cannot acquire each other, and this system should be guided by five pages of principles that ensure transparency and honesty. Recall that the Depression-era Glass-Steagall Act required only 37 pages to set right America's financial institutions. Those 37 pages laid out principles to follow, not detailed instructions.

That is the only way complex systems can be managed: with simple guidelines and principles.

Albert Einstein knew something about complex mathematics and systems, and he famously observed: *"Any intelligent fool can make things bigger and more complex. It takes a touch of genius and a lot of courage to move in the opposite direction."*

That insight will guide our discussion of alternative systems, for the only systems that are sustainable are those that operate according to simple, easily understood principles and guidelines.

If we understand the counterproductive nature of trying to control complex systems with ever-more complex instructions and rules, we understand why expansive government and central planning are doomed to fail: they are ultimately attempts to control complex systems to meet the needs of their vested interests. They will necessarily fail, regardless of how many resources are invested in the attempt.

The only sustainable government is one that is limited to a handful of simple guidelines that it uses to maintain a transparent, honest, level playing field for its citizens.

The Pareto Distribution

We have already discussed diminishing returns, where every additional investment yields less return. Another key concept is the

Pareto Distribution, a "rule of Nature" that is visible in a variety of systems both natural and human-made.

Vilfredo Pareto, an early 20th century Italian economist, found that 80% of the lands in the district were owned by 20% of the populace. This is the basis of the 80/20 rule that says 20% of the sales people generate 80% of the sales, 20% of the pea pods in a garden contain 80% of the peas, etc.

The rule is not precise, of course; it responds to the parameters of the situation. But it is remarkably accurate across a broad range of activities and economics. For example, Pareto's analysis of British tax records found that 70% of the income was earned by 30% of the people. In the U.S., about 80% of Federal income taxes are paid by the top 20%.

The 80/20 rule can be distilled down to the 64/4 rule, as 80% of 80% is 64% and 20% of 20% is 4%. Thus 4% of U.S. households own about 60% of the financial wealth owned by households.

The United Nations Development Program Report found the distribution of global income to be very uneven, with the richest 20% of the world's population controlling 82.7% of the world's income.

Microsoft noted that by fixing the top 20% of the most reported bugs, 80% of the errors and crashes would be eliminated. Researchers have found 80% of the crimes are perpetrated by 20% of the criminals, and that 20% of workplace hazards cause 80% of workplace injuries. About 20% of patients absorb 80% of healthcare costs.

This applies to all sorts of situations. We can estimate that doing the top 20% of a list of 100 ways to improve health will achieve 80% of the potential benefits. In other words, if the optimum exercise regime is walking 100 minutes a day, walking 20 minutes a day will accrue 80% of the health benefits of regular exercise.

In a similar fashion, a dwelling of 600 square feet provides 80% of the utility value of a 3,000 square foot house (20% of 3,000 is 600). The smaller dwelling offers a private bath, kitchen and sleeping quarters, a warm, secure environment, room for storage, and so on—80% of everything we value in a dwelling.

The first 20% offers 80% of the value; the remaining 80% offers diminishing returns. This is a very powerful concept.

Look how many systems in America have it backward. Our healthcare system does very little preventive medicine (the first 20%)

because it's not profitable to do so. Instead, the system waits until people are very sick and then lavishes 80% of the money on them, again because it is profitable to do so.

There is another aspect of the Pareto Distribution (also called the Pareto Principle) called the "vital few." Once 20% of the populace gathers round a firm belief, those few exert an outsized influence on the other 80%.

Once 20% of a neighborhood's homeowners default on their mortgages, this exerts an outsized influence on the value of the other 80%. Since the 80/20 rule can be distilled down to the 64/4 rule, this means that the "vital few" can be as small as 4% of a group.

Back in February, 2007, near the peak of the housing bubble, I wrote an article entitled "Can 4% of Homeowners Sink the Entire Market?" I suggested that once the subprime mortgage defaults reached 4% of the total mortgages (about 2 million defaults out of 50 million mortgages), they would crash the entire housing market—which is precisely what happened.

This shows the power of the "vital few." The Internet was virtually unknown in 1990, with a mere 3 million users globally. Once 4% of American households had an Internet connection—at that time, slow 14.4 modem connections with no web browser—they exerted an outsized influence on 64% of the populace, who learned that there was this amazing new technology called the Internet.

When the first commercial web browser, Netscape Navigator, became available in late 1994, the 4% with an Internet connection quickly rose to 20% in 1997. Once that threshold was reached, the number quickly leaped to over 60% by 2001.

This is an example of how technologies, ideas and beliefs are adopted by a large population. When only 2% of the population has a technology or understands a concept (nowadays, some refer to this as a "meme"), it is a "fringe" movement. If a technology or idea reaches the critical threshold around 4%, however, the users become the "vital few" who influence 64% of the populace. Once the movement has reached 20% of the group, it sets the path that eventually 80% will adopt.

It is critically important to understand this pathway of how new technologies and ideas are adopted. A 'fringe' technology or idea can quickly enter the mainstream once it reaches thresholds of adoption.

Many of the ideas I will present in this section are currently "fringe" ideas. Some will remain on the fringes; others will reach 4%, 20% and then 80% of the populace.

New technologies tend to follow this pattern. For example, in the early 20th century, autos powered by steam, electricity and the internal-combustion engine (ICE) all competed in a nascent marketplace for "horseless carriages." The ICE power train soon won out and was adopted as the industry standard.

The same is true of ideas. Environmental concerns were "fringe" ideas until Rachel Carson's book "The Silent Spring" was published in late 1962. This boosted awareness of the issues to the point that the "vital few" influenced the entire population, culminating in the first "Earth Day" in 1970 that reached the 20% threshold, setting the course for the 80%. Within a few years, laws were passed by consensus that protected "the commons" from dumping and exploitation. In the late 1960s, American rivers were catching fire because they were so polluted with industrial wastes. By the late 1970s, this was no longer the case.

Nowadays, most Americans share the basic values of the environmental movement, though they express the values in varying ways. Those who hunt and fish are in favor of wilderness, clean air and water and seasonal hunting/fishing because these are the foundations of sustainable wildlife. Everyone wants water that doesn't catch fire or come out of the tap a dirty, noxious brown.

At this point in late 2012, relatively few people are aware of some of the ideas presented here. Once 4% of the American populace has embraced a new idea or technology, the "vital few" will introduce the ideas to the broader public. Which technologies and ideas will reach the critical 4% threshold? No one can know which is why I can only provide a sketch of possibilities rather than a roadmap.

If we take the long-term historical perspective, we find that modern global capitalism has gone through many upheavals, each of which saw the dissolution of the old order and the emergence of an even greater source of capital and power.

The S-Curve

Another key model that repeats again and again in Nature and human civilization is the S-curve. Technologies and ideas follow a curve of adoption that is peculiarly similar to the infection rate of new diseases, among other natural phenomena. This path of development traces out a curve that looks like an elongated letter S.

The basic S-curve can be summarized as a series of stages: a long period of initiation (below 4%), followed by emergence (reaches 20%), rapid expansion (reaches 80%), maturity (leveling out above 80%) and finally stagnation (decline or collapse).

The pattern from initiation to stagnation can be seen in the advance of the Black Plague in 14th century Europe and the rise of Internet connections. Underlying similarity is a feature of systems.

In the case of infectious diseases, once the disease has spread throughout the population, those with no immunity die and the survivors have gained immunity. The death rate from the disease quickly declines and collapses.

Social and economic systems also follow the S-curve of adoption, maturity, stagnation and collapse; feudalism stagnated and collapsed and was replaced by an early form of capitalism, which was then replaced by new forms.

If we combine the insights of the Pareto Distribution and the S-Curve, we can see that financialization—the reliance on excessive debt and leverage—has reached stagnation and is about to collapse. We can also see that centralization itself is following an S-Curve and will decline as the decentralizing power of the Internet creatively destroys diminishing-return systems. This includes not only private-sector cartels but the government itself. All government will shrink because it is no longer affordable, productive or sustainable.

The entire structure of American life rests on financialization and centralization, and the demise and replacement of these models is inevitable. This is why things are falling apart: these systems have reached their limits and are stagnating, yielding diminishing returns even as ever-larger sums of money are dumped into them. Though everyone who depends on the Status Quo refuses to accept it, the decline and collapse of these systems is inevitable. That is simply how the world works, and borrowing more money and passing 2,300-page laws cannot stop it.

What can we do about it? We can either resist the inevitable, retreat into denial and be swept away on the tides of history, or we can accept that adaptation is pasrt of life and embrace the inevitable changes sweeping through our economy and society. We can join the 4% who influence the 64%, and become one of the 20% who will influence the 80%. If we rise to the occasion and take responsibility, we can make the inevitable a positive change for ourselves and for our nation.

From Productive to Extractive: Understanding Premiums

People adopt a way of doing things for two basic reasons: one, there is no alternative, and two, if it offers greater benefits than previous ways of doing things.

When a business can charge a higher price because people value its products more than they value competing products, we say that the business can charge a premium. This "extra money" is profit that can be invested in research and development of new products, expansion or distributed to the business owners.

Companies with large profit margins have such strong demand for their products that they can charge a premium. Companies with very thin profit margins have very little premium; their products are "commodities" so similar to competing products that they create no demand strong enough to create a premium.

The other way to obtain a premium is to not allow any other choice. In the classic "company town" serving an isolated mine or plantation, the company only allows one store in town, the one it owns. Since there is no alternative, the company store can charge a premium, what we call an enforced or involuntary premium. Residents would abandon the company store in a heartbeat if a better, cheaper alternative were available, but no competition is allowed, as that would end the company store's fat profits—the premium it charges for being a monopoly.

This is why the highest profit, lowest-risk model of business is monopoly, as a monopoly can charge a huge premium without fear of its customers abandoning it for competitors. In a monopoly or cartel, there are no competitors.

The government is just such a monopoly. It can charge a huge premium for its services because it doesn't allow any competition or alternative. When the government wants more money to fund its operations, it either raises taxes or it borrows the money from future taxpayers, a blatant form of theft. Why should future taxpayers have to pay for services consumed in the present? Since the government is an enforced monopoly, it can borrow money from future taxpayers with impunity.

Here is the important difference between voluntary and involuntary premiums: voluntary premiums are productive: we rapidly adopt a new technology or way of doing things because it is not only faster, better and cheaper, it offers much greater productivity and freedom of choice.

Involuntary premiums do not allow competition or alternatives, and so they are extractive: they are a counterproductive parasite that extracts a premium and gives nothing in return.

The company store doesn't provide better service or some other value for its higher prices: the customers get nothing in return for paying higher prices. All the extra money goes to the monopoly.

When healthcare cartels charge high prices for medical services that cost $1/10^{th}$ as much in other nations, they are charging an involuntary premium because there is no alternative allowed. The primary enforcer of involuntary premiums, the government, has dug regulatory moats around its favored private cartels that do not allow competition, or that create such a high entry cost that potential competitors cannot afford to enter the field.

Just like the residents of the company town, we have no choice but to pay high premiums for poor service and low quality because no alternatives are allowed.

Highly desirable cities can levy high taxes because people recognize the value they are receiving for the premium: the city's taxes are high, but the schools, library, public transport and other city services are superior.

Voluntary premiums must be productive. Involuntary premiums are unproductive and extractive.

Understood in this way, we can see how the entire U.S. economy is layered with extractive, involuntary premiums. This is why so many things have become unaffordable and thus unsustainable. We pay twice as much for healthcare as residents of other nations; we pay high tuition for universities bloated with administration costs, our fighter aircraft are now so costly that we cannot afford them—the list of involuntary, unproductive premiums is endless.

The national surplus isn't large enough to fund all these parasitic premiums, and so the Federal government borrows $1.3 trillion a year, a staggering 35% of its entire budget, to pay for all the friction, waste and unproductive premiums in the Status Quo.

The return on complexity, centralization and monopolies has diminished to less than zero.

Understanding Complexity

Joseph Tainter's 1988 book *The Collapse of Complex Societies* explains how highly successful civilizations such as the Roman Empire collapsed despite their wealth and long success. (Another book with the same theme is *The Upside of Down: Catastrophe, Creativity, and the Renewal of Civilization* by Thomas Homer-Dixon.)

The basic idea here is that increasing complexity is highly productive in the stages of growth from initiation to maturity on the S-curve. Highly productive complexity is the 20% that produces 80% of the benefits.

Examples abound. Long-distance trade is very complex, arduous and risky, yet trading is extraordinarily profitable. As far back as the Roman era, trade between China, India, the Mideast and Europe introduced productive ideas and profitable goods to the great empires of the day.

By the 1500s, trade was creating great surplus (wealth) in Europe that was then reinvested in more trade, manufacturing, art, education, books, and all the other pieces of the Renaissance and modern capitalism.

In the 1800s, complex systems of canals and railroads led to increased trade and productivity. Complex financial systems of stocks, insurance policies, futures options and joint ventures arose in the 1500s and greatly increased the ways risk could be managed and funds could be raised for investment.

Complex systems of electrification, purified water and waste disposal enabled cities to become more livable and productive. Complex systems of communication—telegraph, telephone and the Internet—created new opportunities for higher productivity.

Systems that manage and feed off complexity—what we call bureaucracies—expanded as the surplus grew to the point that extractive premiums could be charged without stopping productive growth.

It's important to remember that much of what we think of as surplus or profit resulted from the extraction of cheap oil and coal. Once the cheap oil has been used up and oil costs more, our surplus shrinks.

The primary involuntary premium is the central government, and back before the fossil-fuel powered industrial revolution created stupendous amounts of surplus, the Federal government was very small. In 1822, the Federal government's budget was 2% of the nation's gross domestic product (GDP), and the total national debt was $98 million, about 12% of the nation's output (GDP).

Now the Federal government is over 25% of the GDP, and local government is another 15%. The national debt is now over 100% of the nation's $15 trillion GDP.

Put another way, The Federal government spent about $30 per person in the 1820s, a number that rose to $129 per person in the 1910s. By the mid-2000s, the Federal budget was over $7,000 per person, and state and local government spending added another $5,000 per person for total government spending of over $12,000 each year.

At least one-third of that Federal spending is borrowed, and a significant part of local government capital spending is funded by bonds (borrowed money).

Why has government expanded to the point that we have to borrow trillions of dollars every year just to keep it afloat? One reason is that extractive bureaucracies work like a ratchet: they happily expand but are incapable of ratcheting down.

Companies that grow large enough to develop massive bureaucracies have the same feature: their bureaucracies rapidly expand when complexity is creating productivity, but when the company's expansion reaches the top of the S-curve and productivity declines, the bureaucracy is incapable of shrinking.

Why is this so? Every bureaucracy and agency came into existence to fulfill a complex function, and every bureaucracy and agency—and every employee in those agencies and bureaucracies—will move Heaven and Earth to justify their existence and staffing levels. Were anyone in these bureaucracies to admit that they'd become an extractive, counterproductive source of friction, then the very existence of the bureaucracy would be called into question.

Rather than admit this and lose their job and perquisites, everyone in bureaucracies constantly seeks to expand their power and regulatory reach, as this justifies their continued existence.

Nobody in regulatory agencies ever convenes a meeting to radically reduce regulations to the point where 20% of the potential regulation provides 80% of the benefits, as this would requires less regulation, fewer staffers and lower budgets. Instead, regulators seek to raise costs by 20% to extract the last 1% of benefit—the very definition of diminishing returns.

Since the government is a monopoly, there is no pressure from alternatives or competition: agencies are free to expand their spending to the limit of their political power, regardless of the counterproductive drag they place on the nation's economy.

When a corporation reaches the stagnation stage on the S-curve and its bloated bureaucracy cannot shrink, the company starts losing vast sums of money and eventually goes out of business. This has happened to corporations that were once shining examples of rapid growth and productivity.

Unfortunately, governments cannot go out of business when they become bloated and counterproductive; they take their entire civilization down with them.

At some point, the ever-increasing burden of more regulation and higher extractive premiums reaches a tipping point where these costs exceed the surplus generated by the economy. At that point, the system implodes.

Since the U.S. has the privilege of the reserve currency and a global military and commercial empire, we think "it can't happen to us." Rest assured that the Romans had the exact same overconfidence in their ability to spend more than they generated in surplus.

Borrowing money to fill the widening gap between what you generate in surplus and what you spend on involuntary premiums is like trying to fool Mother Nature: you think you're getting away with it until your entire house of cards collapses in a chaotic heap.

Let's review the main points here.

Complexity provides a benefit when it enables greater productivity and surplus. But bureaucracies that arise to manage that complexity are like ratchets; they only know how to expand and are incapable of contracting. Complexity thus moves from being productive to being extractive, as it moves from managing rapid growth to protecting bureaucracies that have become unproductively complex. Government bureaucracies charge involuntary premiums that are unrelated to the productivity of the economy; their share of the national income keeps rising even as the economy reaches the decline phase of the S-curve.

Extractive bureaucracies justify their budgets by increasing regulatory complexity to the point that the added complexity acts as a drag on what little productivity remains.

There are two other key characteristics of bureaucratic bloat. One is that making things progressively simpler is not possible in these systems, for two reasons: 1) the bureaucracy would be revealed as a system that can yield positive results by being reduced, the exact opposite of what it wants to happen; and 2) extractive bureaucracies quickly harden into interlocking systems that are immune to simplification and contraction.

This inflexibility leaves these extractive systems vulnerable to diminishing returns and eventual collapse. As surpluses decline, the resources of the bureaucracy are devoted to battling other fiefdoms over the shrinking pie and the bureaucracy's value plummets even further.

What happens when the surplus drops below the cost of all the bureaucracies? The system simplifies by default, not by planning.

Complex regulations are increasingly ignored, both by the citizens and the remaining regulators. The regulations are still on the books, but the system can no longer afford to impose them. When Rome collapsed, there were hundreds of codes, laws and regulations covering every aspect of commerce and life. They were not repealed; they just became irrelevant.

There is another consequence of steadily expanding bureaucracies seeking to justify their budgets. I will illustrate with a true story. A few years ago, an old warehouse was occupied by artists who paid a few hundred dollars a month for their loft spaces. Though it wasn't zoned for residential occupancy, the artists naturally lived in their cheap lofts because they couldn't afford the high rents in the city. Nobody minded because the warehouse was in the old industrial part of town.

Then someone complained to the city that the residents weren't legally entitled to live in their lofts. The city regulators swarmed over the building, issuing code violations left and right. The owner of the building could not afford to meet the requirements, and so the artists were evicted ("you can't fight city hall"), the warehouse was torn down and replaced by luxury condominiums costing hundreds of thousands of dollars each.

The old warehouse probably had some safety issues—never mind the occupants had lived there without incident for decades. The point is regulatory agencies have no way to recognize that "good enough" yields enormous benefits—in this case, preserving very low-cost housing.

From the Pareto Distribution we can estimate that spending a mere 4% of the potential safety renovation budget would have reaped 64% of the safety benefits, as the most glaring deficiencies are the cheapest and easiest to address: strengthening handrails, installing smoke and CO_2 alarms, providing fire extinguishers, adding plywood shear walls, and so on. Spending 20% would have yielded 80% of the potential safety gain. Yet the current regulatory system recognizes only 100% as sufficient: all codes and regulations must be met or the owners are in violation.

As a result, a luxury building was the only project that could be built because the cost of meeting all the regulations was incredibly high.

This is America now, on so many levels: by the time all the regulations have been met and all the complexity paid for, the cost is higher than all but a few can afford. We have regulated and complexized ourselves into permanent unaffordability.

Since our interlocking bureaucracies cannot shrink, we are filling the widening gap between our surplus and our bloated cost basis with vast sums of borrowed money. This is the path to financial ruin and collapse.

Complexity as a Moat

Here is the "problem" that centralized complexity "solves": it protects State fiefdoms and private-sector cartels from competition and inquiry. Fiefdoms and cartels have one goal: self-preservation. Once sufficient power and wealth is concentrated in a cartel, its power can be devoted to self-preservation.

Self-preservation becomes the primary goal.

Complexity works beautifully as self-preservation, because it actually expands the bureaucratic power of fiefdoms and widens the moat protecting cartels. Once the bureaucracy expands to manage all those new rules, only a handful of corporations can possibly afford the regulatory reporting burdens. They are then free to exploit the populace as a "legal" cartel.

In the competition with the private sector for scarce capital, the State always wins. That's why banana republics are characterized by bloated, unaccountable State bureaucracies and the systemic corruption of sweetheart deals, no-bid contracts, shadow banking, inefficient workforces that cannot be fired, and so on.

Complexity offers the façade of facsimile "reforms" that end up expanding the agency's powers. The result is system that is so complex that it loses all accountability. Complexity is the perfect moat.

This is the idea, of course: banana republics and other neofeudal societies always manage to support sprawling, counterproductive State bureaucracies and private cartels.

But complexity does have an eventual cost: collapse. Keep adding decks to the ship and eventually it capsizes and sinks. One the ship is sufficiently top-heavy, all it takes is a small wave to capsize it.

Complexity and Information Asymmetry

Complexity lends itself to information asymmetry, a primary tool of government and corporate dominance. I mentioned information asymmetry earlier, in the example of a global corporation taking control of a town's water supply: the corporation knows everything there is no know about the town and its water resources, while the town knows only what the corporation chooses to reveal about its real plans and strategies.

How much information is there in 10,000 pages of corporate filings or 2,000 pages of statutes? At first glance, we would say there is a mountain of information in these complexity thickets, but upon reflection we would soon conclude this apparent wealth of information is illusory: without vast resources and the insider knowledge needed to decode the thousands of pages, no one can extract the key passages or grasp the ramifications of the mass of data. In effect, there is no information in these voluminous documents because the real goals, plans, agendas, strategies and consequences are hidden by the sheer size and complexity of the documents.

This is how corporations and government agencies create information asymmetry: those who draft the documents know precisely what's important and what's been hidden in the depths that will benefit the political/financial Aristocracy.

Information asymmetry is a very powerful concept. It basically means those who hold the information have an insurmountable advantage over those who don't.

Here is an example of how information asymmetry works. In the pre-Internet days, only the airline knew how many seats were booked and how many were open on any flight. The knowledge was 100% asymmetrical; the passengers had no knowledge and the airline had 100% of the information. As a result, they could charge a passenger in one seat $250 while the person in the next seat might have paid only $150.

Information asymmetry enables control and high profits. The Internet is destroying information asymmetry and as a result it is lowering costs. Airlines have a much more difficult time maintaining Information asymmetry when the price of seats is available to anyone with an Internet connection; the asymmetry has dropped, and so have prices.

Another form of information asymmetry is based on cost and access. In the 1960s, computers were so costly to buy and operate that only a few big companies and government agencies could afford them. Access to these costly assets was strictly limited.

The knowledge of how to build rockets capable of reaching the atmosphere was limited to NASA and the Soviet Union's space agency; it was too costly for any other agency to develop.

Now that computational power is cheap, the engineering has become affordable, and an important threshold was recently reached: a commercially developed U.S. rocket lifted a government payload into orbit because the private-sector rocket launch was faster and cheaper than any equivalent NASA launch.

Two-Way Communication and Adding an Information Loop

What is the difference between productive and extractive systems? One key difference is the voluntary, productive system enables two-way communication between producers and customers, while the unproductive extractive system has only one-way communication.

Behind closed doors, in the shadow systems of governance where regulations are crafted, corporate cartel representatives meet with lawmakers' staffers to describe what they want in the way of regulatory moat to protect their profits and power. The staffers bury the key parts in the hundreds of pages of complexity.

Customers and citizens affected by the new statutes are given a for-public-relations-only opportunity to publicly comment on the voluminous regulations. They are dutifully thanked for their input and their comments are placed in File 13, also known as the trash can.

In the private sector, companies that have no information loop from their customers eventually go out of business. Unfortunately, cartels and the government pay lip-service to customer feedback but their extractive systems are founded on one-way communication: they tell us what to do and what to pay.

As these top-heavy extractive systems fray and collapse under their own weight, sustainable replacement systems will add information loops from users, customers and citizens to enable meaningful two-way communication and interaction.

Scientist Donella H. Meadows (B.S. in chemistry, PhD in Biophysics) described how adding information feedback loops can change entire systems in her seminal essay, *Leverage Points: Places to Intervene in A System*, and her book *Thinking in Systems*.

Much of what we now consider regulation that has to be managed by centralized government will be crowdsourced and operated more like interactive web-based services, where customer satisfaction and transparent information are the key regulatory determinants of behavior.

We will discuss these new decentralized, distributed, "free" models of regulation later.

Understanding Local/Global Optimizations

We discussed voluntary, productive premiums, where customers choose to pay a premium for the added value and benefit provided, and involuntary, extractive premiums levied by "company stores," cartels and government.

Voluntary trade has created wealth since the first human groups generated surplus to trade. (Involuntary trade is called conquest.) How does trade create wealth? The principle is called comparative advantage, meaning that one group trades its surplus to another group in exchange for its surplus, to their mutual benefit.

If I'm creating a surplus of grain locally, the local price is low due to supply and demand: supply exceeds demand, and nobody wants to pay a premium for something that is in local abundance. If I ship the surplus grain to a distant land that is suffering from a grain shortage, my surplus will fetch a high price. That locale might have some local products which I can buy cheap and bring home to sell for a profit.

The key concept here is that some good or service that is optimized somewhere else (that is, produced cheaply and in abundance) will fetch a profit when transported to a locale where it is not yet optimized.

This is an oversimplification, of course, but the point is that any local advantage due to shortage will attract supply from elsewhere to take advantage of the potential for outsized profit.

Optimized local production will become the global optimization as it displaces local inefficiencies.

Consider computer microprocessors as an example. At one time, various countries were designing and manufacturing microprocessors. The chips were costly to manufacture and so the price was high locally. Once Intel produced a chip that was faster, better and cheaper, it moved from being the local optimization in San Jose, California, to the global optimization for all Windows-based computers.

At one time, designing and coding software required a lot of programming. Programmers were optimized for their local area, meaning they could charge more if their services were in demand and programmers were scarce in their locale.

With the advent of the Internet and automated software tools, many basic programming projects such as coding web pages can be accomplished from any Internet connection with free or nearly free tools.

These solutions and tools quickly become the global optimization.

Enterprises everywhere on the planet must constantly adopt the latest global optimizations or they will lose their competitive advantage, and customers will migrate elsewhere.

Here is an example of network optimization. In the old days, the local store could charge a premium because it was the only place that had the part you wanted in stock. Now you can order the part from a central distributor, a distant parts shop or even an individual and have it delivered for a modest cost within a few days.

The lowest-cost provider in the network becomes not just the lowest-cost provider in that locale but everywhere in the network.

This is a process that the Internet has expanded exponentially as the number of "nodes" in the network expands from the local parts supplier to thousands of suppliers.

This optimization is one driver of the "end of work" we discussed earlier, as local advantages are quickly eliminated by global optimizations.

Monopolies, cartels and governments have no competition, and so they are immune to the pressure of global optimizations—at least until they collapse under their own weight.

Local Optimizations That Remain Local

Local optimizations can remain local for two basic reasons: 1) the residents choose to support local enterprises rather than support global corporations that provide cheaper commodity products, and 2) the goods or services cannot be made elsewhere and delivered to the local area.

Fresh-baked bread cannot be delivered very far before it is no longer fresh-baked.

A bottled beer can be shipped around the world and delivered to your doorstep, but the social atmosphere in a local micro-brewery cannot be "manufactured" elsewhere and shipped. Each micro-brewery in a locale can fashion its own optimization, and these similar but different optimizations can create more interest and revenues than a single commodity brewer.

Commodities can be shipped around the world and digital services are a mouse-click away anywhere on Earth. But a home-cooked meal, a haircut, a word of comfort and much else is intrinsically local.

The advent of 3-D printing and local computerized fabrication means that global solutions—open-system software and the technology of desktop fabrication—are localized: decentralized and distributed. The raw materials and energy may well be produced in centralized plants, but the value-added part of manufacturing can be highly localized.

In other words, in distributed, decentralized systems, the global optimization may be local.

Section Six:
What We Can Do About It

This book is titled "why things are falling apart and what we can do about it," and at long last we have come to the "what we can do about it," the solutions.

Let's start by recalling the Status Quo is falling apart not because of individual wrong-doing or incompetence, but because the entire centralized Status Quo is unaffordable and unsustainable.

Tweaking policies cannot fix what's broken: the entire system is broken, on all the levels we have covered. The Status Quo based on centralization, self-serving vested interests, a financial Aristocracy, friction, malinvestment, officially sanctioned bribery, debt, leverage, perception management, central planning, promises that cannot be kept, shadow systems of finance and governance, crony capitalism, an authoritarian government that protects parasitic cartels, fiefdoms and monopolies, tyranny of the majority and a consumerist society that is short on well-being and long on alienation cannot survive. It will fray, weaken and collapse in insolvency.

We cannot know the precise flow of history over the next decade or two, but we do know the centralized model that relies on ever-expanding debt to mask fundamental financial insolvency is doomed.

There are only two possible ends to the centralized model of ever-expanding debt: repudiation of the State's gargantuan debts or destruction of the nation's currency, i.e. national impoverishment. There are no other possibilities, for all the reasons we have covered in depth.

The expansive Central State is on an S-curve of decline, and this is most apparent in nations that cannot borrow a trillion dollars a year to fund an unsustainable Status Quo like the U.S. As noted before, all government is a claim on national surpluses. As those surpluses decline, government must shrink accordingly. Unfortunately, the Status Quo system is like a ratchet: it only knows how to expand, and contraction will trigger systemic failure.

This is Peak Government.

Those who depend on a strategy of pleading with central authorities to continue funding at old levels are doomed to disappointment. These systems are following an S-Curve of rapid expansion, stagnation and decline. Breaking the mindset that Central State subsidies are the solution to every problem is difficult, but clinging to failed models of the past is not the way forward.

The Outline of a Replacement System:
Decentralized, Adaptive, Transparent, Accountable

Decentralized, distributed, networked systems that enable the free exchange of digital capital and innovative models will replace the centralized control model because they create systems and solutions that are faster, better, cheaper, adaptable and sustainable.

Centralized models of finance and governance are parasitic and unproductive, and so they will collapse and be replaced by some new arrangement that is simpler, cheaper and sustainable.

I call this the DATA model: Decentralized, Adaptive, Transparent, Accountable.

Investing resources in high-yield solutions is the winning strategy, not just in the U.S. but globally. Investing the 20% that yields 80% of the benefits is the only sustainable path forward.

What is the goal of the DATA model? Radically lower the cost of living and completely reorder our understanding of prosperity. If we radically lower the cost basis of the "good life," then it automatically becomes accessible to everyone willing to participate, contribute and reciprocate.

The Principles of a Replacement/Alternative System

The DATA model (Decentralized, Adaptive, Transparent, Accountable) will not suddenly replace the centralized model. It will develop as an open alternative system, rapidly evolving and adapting as the centralized model crumbles and fails. Note that the DATA model is the exact opposite of the Status Quo system, which is centralized, mal-adaptive, opaque and unaccountable.

As noted before, complex systems cannot be controlled with complex instructions issued by centralized authorities. Complex systems evolve and adapt according to a limited number of simple principles.

The DATA model starts with this very limited set of principles:

1. Individual honesty and integrity, Institutional honesty and integrity. A nation of dishonest people cannot expect honest institutions or transactions. Honesty is the bedrock of the common good and social order. Unfortunately, centralized institutions place a premium on complicity (silence when fiction is presented as fact), withholding information that threatens vested interests, misrepresentation, perception management and a host of other actions in the spectrum of dishonesty.

The honest person will thus pay a price for being honest within an institution that relies on dishonesty to protect itself and maintain its premium. Fortunately, the alternative to centralized institutions is distributed, decentralized systems based on referral, trust, verification, transparency, reciprocity and voluntary opt-in. These alternative systems are based not on "rights" but on privilege: being a member is a privilege, not a right, and a privilege can be withdrawn if the member abuses the system or takes advantage of other members.

As Eric Hoffer noted, "we lie the loudest when we lie to ourselves."

2. Transparency, information symmetry. Interested parties all have access to the same information.

3. Two-way communication between organizations and participants, open feedback loops that can easily be added.

4. Voluntary, transparent opt-in organizations and enterprises.

5. Membership is a privilege with responsibilities and accountability, not a right. The only rights are the civil liberties guaranteed by the Bill of Rights, what the Declaration of Independence summarized as the rights to life, liberty and the pursuit of happiness.

Examples of voluntary opt-in organizations include:

- Formal membership with ownership or labor commitments: housing co-ops, co-housing, co-operatives

- Formal membership, access not ownership: car sharing (Zipcar, Wheelz, etc.), community gardens, tool lending libraries
- Financial: crowd-funding, micro-loans, micro-investing.
- Educational: Kahn Institute, free courses.
- Informal: forums, review/customer feedback sites, social media.
- Career/Enterprise: LinkedIn, guilds, professional groups.
- Participatory: crowd-sourced regulation, open-source software development, local community projects.

Many of the functions we think of as exclusively governmental could be performed by networked voluntary groups. Many of the services we think of as exclusively institutional such as healthcare can be performed by decentralized organizations.

6. Self-sufficiency, what Simon Hodges calls "off the centralized grid." The less a community, enterprise or household depends on increasingly complex and fragile centralized systems, the more resilient, self-reliant and prosperous they are. Self-reliance is the result of decentralization, adaptability, accountability and transparency.

What happens when these systems are allowed to evolve and adapt is that costs can often be reduced by an order of magnitude: what once cost $100 now costs $10. This is especially true if the value of "good enough"—that the vital 20% investment can yield 80% of the benefit—is rewarded within the system.

Faster, Better, Cheaper with ESSA:
Eliminate, Simplify, Standardize, Automate

The centralized Status Quo's "solution" to a rising cost basis due to fraud, friction, debt and malinvestment is to borrow even more money so it can continue to do more of what has already failed.

What is unsustainably costly and complex will be replaced by a new arrangement, one way or another, so we might as well choose a positive outcome by embracing the DATA model and a radical reduction in complexity and cost. We can start with ESSA: eliminate, simplify, standardize, automate.

Here are two examples of ESSA on a large scale.

1. Eliminate income taxes and all tax returns. How could this be done? Replace income and payroll taxes with a consumption tax the end-buyer pays on all goods and services. Replace income taxes on investment/speculative income with a transaction tax on every financial transaction: buying or selling stocks, bonds, derivatives, mortgages and every other financial instrument on any market.

This would eliminate the tax preparation industry, the tax loophole industry, most of the IRS and all the millions of hours of labor and billions of dollars currently wasted on preparing tax returns.

With taxes collected on final sales and financial transactions only, only providers would have to account for the fees collected on sales.

This eliminates corporate taxes, too. Corporate profits eventually flow to individual shareholders, who then pay the consumption tax when they buy goods or services.

This is not something tax accountants would favor, but it is the sort of solution that will eventually replace a system that is nothing but opportunities for fraud, waste and malinvestment.

2. Eliminate the current "sickcare" and Medicare/Medicaid systems and replace them with cash only care and voluntary catastrophic insurance. Although this is considered "impossible," this was the norm in postwar America.

Recall that roughly 80% of all medical expenses are spent on 20% of patients. If we looked deeper, we would probably find that roughly 60% of all costs were spent on 4% chronically ill patients (the 80/20, 64/4 rules). This suggests that 80% of healthcare could be handled by cash-only care that focused on prevention and honesty.

As we all know, people who have virus-caused colds often demand antibiotics, even though these don't work on viruses. Obliging doctors and nurses give in and prescribe antibiotics, which not only don't work on colds, they dilute the effectiveness of the antibiotics when they're actually needed.

As a nation committed to the DATA model, the answer given to patients demanding useless costly medications is "no."

What few people seem to understand is that the availability of student loans has enabled college costs to skyrocket 700%. If there were no student loans, universities would either find a way to provide education faster, better and cheaper for what people could afford or they would go out of business.

The same is true of healthcare insurance. Without insurance payments, providers would have to find ways to provide care that people could afford. That would drive care towards cheap, highly effective prevention and away from costly, often counterproductive care.

Without insurance to fund fraud (an estimated 40% of Medicare is fraud, though nobody knows because the program is never audited), waste, duplication, friction and malinvestment, care costs would plummet to what people could afford. "Good enough" would become acceptable, and the system would strive to invest the 20% that reaped 80% of the benefit.

Roughly 40% of healthcare costs in America result from paper-shuffling, and another large percentage is consumed by insurance fraud, duplication, defensive medicine and other types of friction and malinvestment. Going to a cash-only system with voluntary catastrophic coverage would instantly eliminate more than half the system's current costs. That's over $1 trillion in savings at the very first pass.

3. Replace $300 million apiece fighter aircraft with $3 million drones that can outfly the enemy's $30 million aircraft and eliminate pilot risk. The enormous investment in pilots would be conserved as pilots would not be lost. Combat losses would be inexpensive and easy to replace.

This is a 100-fold decrease in the cost of weapons. Each generation of military hardware and tactics should improve the effectiveness while reducing costs and risks to personnel.

These are just three examples out of hundreds or perhaps thousands.

Remember, preserving the unaffordable and unsustainable is not an option: the only choice is to watch the tides wash over the Status Quo sand castle or embrace replacement systems that are 1/10th the cost and twice as effective.

Faster, Better, Cheaper with Technology

As of November 2012, a Raspberry Pi computer with 700 MHz CPU with 256 MB RAM costs $25. This does not include a keyboard or monitor, but this computer can power all sorts of devices, large and small, in addition to being a conventional personal computer.

This fully functional and quite powerful computer costs less than a child's kit of interlocking plastic building blocks.

As of this writing, fully functional computer tablets running open-source Linux cost $35 to $45 in China.

Some years ago technology enthusiasts were anticipating the convergence of the computer and the television. Not only have these two devices converged, so have a number of other consumer electronics technologies. Young people have a laptop or tablet computer and a smart phone, and this minimal gear replaces a landline telephone, GPS device, e-book reader, TV, desktop computer, stereo system, cabinet of music CDs and film DVDs and shelves of books. These mobile devices have eliminated entire industries that designed and manufactured myriad devices and storage media.

An entire roomful of expensive electronics has been consolidated into two small devices.

Just as Craigslist wiped out the newspaper industry's cash cow, the classified ad, mobile computing has radically reduced the cost and size of media and media-related devices.

This has led to a consolidation of physical space. Enterprises large and small no longer need office space. Indeed, some new global companies have no headquarters or offices at all; their staff work from home, cafes, or wherever they choose.

Some "incubator" cafes in cities like San Francisco rent conference rooms above the café for people who normally work and meet in the café but who need a private room on occasion.

The whole paradigm of needing a costly and separate home, office and "third space" (not home or work, for example, a favorite café) is consolidating into one space or a shared space.

This new way of working and living reduces costs by 50% or more on the very first pass.

Here is another model for localized optimization of global technologies. Let's say a town or community invests in a publicly accessible workshop equipped with 3-D printing and desktop fabrication machine tools. Residents can use the tools once they become members (accept rules of conduct, fees, share in maintenance, etc.). One key principle is membership is a privilege, not a right. Those who refuse to reciprocate or who engage in dishonesty or fraud are expelled and shunned.

Voluntary organizations require membership, and membership entails responsibilities. Since 4% of any group tends to create 64% of the conflicts and problems, a group must have the right and mechanism to eject the irresponsible and the unaccountable from the group.

The members pay a nominal fee to use the tools, and they pay for the raw materials they consume. Whatever they make is theirs to keep.

Since the cost of computer chips and parts continues to decline, it may soon be cheaper to fabricate a mobile phone case and snap in the chipset, screen and SIMM card yourself. A member might come in and fabricate a cell phone for herself, or she might make a hundred and sell them as part of her micro-enterprise.

The community investment in the workshop would yield a variety of benefits. Entrepreneurs would have access to tools they could not afford on their own, young people could learn valuable skills, and the local economy would benefit from the emergence of micro-enterprises, some of which might expand.

This is simply one example of many of how technology can radically lower costs while benefitting household incomes and the community.

Faster, Better, Cheaper with Behavioral Changes

It's easy to become enamored with technology driven innovations and overlook zero-cost or extremely low-cost behavioral changes.

For example, it is estimated that 5% of household electricity in the U.S. is lost to energizing computers, television and other appliances that are turned off but on standby, as a result of poorly designed standby circuitry.

According to The U.S. Department of Energy, there are 2,776 electrical generation plants in the U.S. That means 140 power plants do nothing but generate the electricity wasted by zombie DVD players, TVs and computers plugged into wall sockets while not in use. One easy solution: put as many of these devices as is practical on power strips which can be turned off with one switch.

If three individuals who each paid a premium for their own apartment share one dwelling, their costs decline by one-third to two-thirds in one pass.

If five households share one vehicle and use public transport, their cost of vehicle ownership drops 80% on the first pass.

This model is based on having access to tools, transport and other amenities without having to pay the enormous premium of owning them all: access not ownership. Sharing costly equipment and space immediately lowers the cost basis of every participant/member by a significant percentage.

Even where ownership is desirable, sharing can radically lower the cost of ownership.

If single-family homes cost $300,000 in area, it is likely that a ten-unit apartment building will cost around $1 million. If ten households form a co-op and buy the ten-unit building, each flat is $100,000, and the maintenance, tools, etc. associated with ownership can all be shared, lowering the cost of ownership further.

In Bangkok, Thailand, streets that have been designated pedestrian-only host three different sets of vendors. In the morning, coffee and breakfast vendors set up. Mid-day, lunch and snack vendors take over the street. In the evening, fruit sellers and a full range of clothing and other vendors set up shop. This one street supports three different sets of vendors, in a lively and safe environment.

Note that none of these radical reductions in cost basis require any new technology. They are all behavioral.

Very modest investments aimed at improving the experience of pedestrians and bicycle riders can yield substantial benefits. Closing the downtown blocks for weekend street fairs attracts large audiences for shop owners and provides free fun for families and the community.

A small sum invested in pavement restriping and barriers creates safe bike lanes that boost bicycle use, improving health and air quality while removing vehicles from the road. Studies have found that the young professionals who bring energy, innovation and earning power are drawn to bicycle-friendly communities. Making modest investments in pedestrian and bicycle friendly urbanism can yield large and enduring benefits to the entire community on a number of fronts.

Once again, these are only a few of hundreds of examples and possibilities where a small "vital" investment yields outsized, sustainable returns.

Regulations, Self-Interest and Incentives

Let's begin our discussion of regulation by comparing several common examples.

Why do we all stop at four-way stop signs? Is it because there is a police officer ready to ticket us at every intersection? No, it is not enforcement that motivates us to obey this law. We rightly fear that breaking the rule will lead to completely avoidable bodily injury and damage to our vehicle.

In other words, it is self-interest which guides our compliance with a common-sense rule that benefits all participants.

Recycling is an ordinance in many communities; we're supposed to recycle for the good of the community and planet. Yet who are the most dedicated recyclers? Those individuals who collect recyclables because there is a small cash premium paid for them.

This example suggests that enforcement is unnecessary if incentives for what benefits the community and the common good are in place and disincentives are in place for what harms the community/common good.

Let's consider an industry that could potentially pollute the environment. In the current Status Quo, there are regulations enforced by the government to punish any polluting activity by the industry.

What if the government shrinks to the point that it is unable to enforce its thousands of regulations?

Could the networked voluntary community offer a substitute model of regulation?

Suppose companies realized that the networked community valued their compliance with common-sense environmental regulations, and that their compliance created a competitive advantage while non-compliance triggered boycotts and an online explosion of bad publicity that eventually hurt sales and profits.

Compliance would then be in the company's self-interest, even if the government's enforcement capacity dwindles or disappears.

Consider the possibility that voluntary monitors could snap a photo with their mobile phone of non-compliance and distribute it in seconds to the network.

Refusing to buy a corporation's goods and services is a cost-free leverage point.

Which is the more likely winning strategy? For the company to accept voluntary monitoring by citizens as a positive for public relations and perhaps the bottom line, or for the company to stonewall citizen regulators and make everyone suspect they have something to hide?

Anyone with any PR and marketing experience knows that Option #2—stonewalling and resistance—is a terribly unprofitable and damaging strategy.

Will regulation vanish if the government shrinks to a shadow of its current size? Not necessarily. The "enforcement" possibilities of open-source technology, voluntary monitoring and networked consumer boycotting are as yet unexplored but undoubtedly significant.

Every enterprise that hopes to be sustainable and profitable understands its customers are its most important partners.

I know this is very controversial, but consider the abject failure of the "war on drugs," which has attempted to apply the 1920s Prohibition of alcohol to marijuana and other "hard" drugs such as cocaine and morphine. Not only has this attempt to suppress drug distribution and use failed miserably, as every drug is available practically everywhere, but it has spawned an unsustainably costly prison system that excels in churning out hardened criminals. The "war on drugs" has also created global drug cartels whose wealth and power now exceed those of some nation-states.

It is instructive to consider the example of Prohibition in the 1920s. By all accounts, Prohibition was the most catastrophic public policy of the 20th century. It spawned and enriched criminal gangs and the Mafia; it led to widespread disregard of the law and to dangerous "bathtub gin" concoctions, and it added a taboo to alcohol consumption that actually increased its attraction.

When one-third or one-half of a nation's adults are routinely breaking the law, then what does the law mean?

The disastrous experiment in attempting to modify people's potentially destructive behavior with brute-force enforcement failed on every count and created horrific unintended consequences.

There is no doubt that alcohol is an exceedingly dangerous drug that causes tens of thousands of deaths every year from vehicle accidents, murder, domestic violence, suicide, alcoholism and from mixing legal prescription drugs with alcohol. Another legal drug, nicotine, also causes tens of thousands of deaths annually.

Legal synthetic heroin sold as prescription painkillers is now a major addictive drug. Criminalizing one drug and then legalizing a synthetic version has simply shifted the use and abuse to the "legal" drug.

Interestingly, marijuana, cocaine and morphine were all legal drugs in the late 19th century. Somehow the country survived these drugs being freely available. Indeed, doctors often prescribed medications whose active ingredient was cannabis. (If you doubt this, you can look it up on the Web.)

The number of deaths that have been judicially attributed to marijuana is near-zero, i.e. statistical noise. (You can also look this up if you doubt it.)

All drugs have negative consequences when abused, but some are more destructive than others. Alcohol, a "legal" but controlled drug, is a deadly, dangerous drug. But very few people go to prison for abusing alcohol—they only go to prison for killing or harming someone while under the influence of alcohol. In general, regulations concerning the consumption of alcohol are punished with fines, and abuse of alcohol is dealt with as an addiction or medical issue. This is also true of nicotine addiction.

This disconnect between the way we understand and deal with deadly "legal" drugs and the way we have attempted to brute-force prohibit "illegal" drugs is striking. Since Prohibition of alcohol failed completely, why are we surprised that the Prohibition of marijuana and other once-legal drugs has also failed miserably? In private, law enforcement officials will concede this failure, but they rarely say so publicly, fearing public and official disapproval. Stating that "The Emperor has no clothes" is never popular with those who have loudly proclaimed the imaginary clothing magnificent.

Once governments shrink, there will no surplus resources to continue the "war on drugs," so we might as well accept its demise.

Illegal drugs appeal to those seeking massive quick profits, those pursuing self-medication, young people seeking taboos to break and those with few positive alternatives in life. A vibrant community that offered work that was meaningful to people in the community would offer a positive alternative. Once every drug was treated like alcohol, legal but controlled, much of the taboo mystique would vanish.

Once marijuana was no longer prohibited and it was legal to grow one's own, the price would drop in price to the point that no drug cartel could charge a premium for it. Once the cost fell, crime created by marijuana distribution and use would plummet as well.

We somehow survived marijuana, cocaine and morphine being legal in the 19th century, and we have somehow survived the legality and common-sense control of alcohol and nicotine, two addictive drugs that directly cause tens of thousands of deaths every year.

This suggests we will survive the legality of marijuana with less loss of life than we have with legal alcohol, legal prescription drugs and tobacco.

Once again we can turn to the Pareto Distribution to aid our understanding. It seems very likely that 20% of the populace accounts for 80% of the drug abuse, and that 4% of the populace accounts for 64% of the abuse. We need to accept that human beings have an innate capacity for self-destructive behavior, and all that we can do with limited resources is offer incentives for positive behavior and disincentives for negative behavior within a regulatory system that recognizes drugs should be controlled but legal and that addiction and abuse are medical issues rather than criminal issues.

The Status Quo has tried to limit the destructive consequences of drug abuse for over 100 years by trying to limit the availability and supply of drugs. This has failed for the simple reason that supply will arise to meet demand. The only solution is to lower demand with better choices and education.

People with productive, socially fulfilling lives have no interest in abusing alcohol, nicotine, cocaine or heroin, and indeed, these products could be free and they would walk past them without a thought. Facing temptation with self-control is a key trait of adulthood, and the only real solution to drug abuse is to reduce demand by creating a society that offers a wealth of opportunities for productive, socially fulfilling lives. Attempting to reduce supply is a fool's game that has squandered billions of dollars, enriched criminal gangs and fostered a destructive war-on-drugs-prison complex that churns out hardened criminals.

The absurdly costly and diminishing-return "war on drugs" will not survive the coming contraction in government spending, for its return on investment is not just marginal, it is negative. Punitive schemes like the "war on drugs" operated by the State will founder as the high-cost State founders. Adding regulatory complexity and cost will only hasten the collapse of the entire system.

The cogent question is always: how can we reap 80% of the benefits with 20% of the investment?

The answer requires looking at the mix of government, market and community and at new models of regulation based on crowd-sourcing, self-interest, simple positive incentives and freely available accurate information.

The Central State's insolvency will open up much-needed space for new models of regulation that do not require punitive punishments or costly enforcement and judiciary systems. As with many other ideas mentioned in this section, these new models have yet to emerge. New technologies and new social arrangements are enabling decentralized, distributed models to evolve that are faster, better and cheaper than the centralized, costly models they will replace.

Restoring the Balance of Government, Community and the Marketplace

Community is by definition decentralized; central government is by definition centralized. The open marketplace of real capitalism is efficient in the allocation of labor, productive assets and capital and therefore productive; crony capitalism of vested interests, cartels and protected fiefdoms is inefficient and unproductive.

We have seen that centralization inevitably leads to involuntary premiums being extracted from the productive economy to prop up unproductive, parasitic monopolies, cartels and fiefdoms.

The Central State extracts involuntary premiums and distributes them to favored vested interests. The community and the decentralized open marketplace are based on voluntary premiums chosen by customers and members of voluntary, self-organizing local communities.

Local communities and small enterprise are intrinsically distributed; the Central State and its favored monopolies and cartels are centralized, protected by complexity moats and supported by involuntary premiums extracted from the productive.

The centralized, concentrated-wealth-and-power model has hollowed out America's economy and society and bled its productive sectors of talent and capital.

If we had to summarize what we can do to fix our economy and society, the answer is restore the balance of government, community and the marketplace. The current Status Quo is based on Central State control of the community and marketplace; concentrations of wealth and power (financialization and vested interests) rule the Central State which rules the entire economy and society.

To restore the necessary role of community and marketplace, the economy and society must be decentralized and political and financial power must be widely distributed.

The present burden of unproductive, costly, extractive complexity is the result of centralized financial arbitrage on a global scale: financialization has transferred wealth from the productive to the financial sector.

Put another way, the Central State and its favored Elites have imposed parasitic premiums on the economy with centrally planned complexity. Their attempt to manage a complex economy with ever-more complex regulations has led to an increasingly financialized and fragile economy that now relies on fudged data, skyrocketing debt and artifice (perception management) to keep from collapsing.

But an economy based on central planning, gross inefficiency, parasitic extraction, financial slight-of-hand, debt, leverage, complexity, diminishing returns, high cost basis, low savings, manufactured "good news" and an obsession with ostentatious consumption is not sustainable, nor can it be fair, free or just.

The Limitations of the Marketplace

In terms of large scale systems, the marketplace is now dominated by State-mandated monopolies and cartels. The largest expenses for most households are their mortgage (the mortgage industry is 98% backed by the government and dominated by the five "too big to fail" banks), healthcare (controlled by the government, dominated by insurance and provider cartels) and higher education (funded by government-backed student loans, grants and research, colleges operate as a State-funded cartel).

The essence of cartel-crony capitalism is that competition is eliminated by decree or by regulatory moats. Power is consolidated in the Central State which then grants monopolies to cartels and favored vested interests.

Industries that are lightly regulated such as computers and the Internet thrive due to lively competition; industries that are tightly regulated by the State are burdened by friction, fraud and diminishing returns. (Recall that 40% of Medicare expenditures are estimated to be fraudulent in some way.)

The obvious advantages of an open market has led many to believe that the competitive marketplace is the "one size fits all solution" to all problems. While a competitive market offers efficiency in many situations, it is not a solution in all situations. The reason is that the market exists to reap a profit, and many situations offer no profit potential.

Adding bikeways to a community offers no profit potential unless users were charged for using the bikeway. There is no profit potential in picking up litter around a neighborhood, unless residents agreed to pay a fee for litter collection.

The market aims to charge a premium for every aspect of life.

Consider the ideal American lifestyle of a 3,000 square-foot single family home occupied by two adults and a child. Daycare, enrichment and/or private schooling costs $2,000 a month; assisted-living care of an elderly parent costs $5,000 a month; the mortgage on the expansive home costs $3,000 a month; property taxes are $1,000 a month; the two vehicles the family needs to commute to work cost $1,500 a month for loan payments, fuel and maintenance; eating out every meal or consuming packaged meals at home costs $1,000 a month; yard and maid service and other domestic services cost $500 a month, and so on. The high income required to pay for all these costs is heavily taxed, so at least $3,000 a month is paid in income and sales taxes.

The market provides the credit, goods and services for every aspect of this idealized life; the community provides nothing and in fact does not exist in this market-dominated lifestyle.

The only problem with this "market provides every solution" lifestyle is that only 10% of the populace can afford it. As incomes continue decaying for the reasons described in previous sections, this could soon decline to 5%.

A "solution" that only works for the top 5% of the populace is not a solution.

The government "solution" is to redistribute income from the top 20% who pay 80% of the income tax to the lower-income households to fund the primary services the high-earners pay on their own: daycare, after-school care, school lunches, healthcare (Medicaid), housing (Section 8) and food (SNAP program, previously known as food stamps).

The problem with the government's redistribution "solution" is that the government is basically borrowing 35% to 40% of every dollar. As we have seen, the demographic tidal wave of retiring Baby Boomers and the "end of paid work" will lower tax revenues while simultaneously increasing expenditures. This double-whammy will capsize the government's borrow-and-spend "solution."

Neither the market nor the Central State "solutions" are sustainable.

That leaves the community as the only real solution.

The Forgotten Foundation of the Economy and Society: Community

We have seen that neither the marketplace nor the Central State can sustainably supply "the good life" to the majority of citizens, for a number of systemic reasons. Both the market and the State have gained power by replacing the non-market economy—what I call the community—with high-cost "solutions" that require ever-increasing amounts of credit, income and tax revenues. Now that incomes are declining and credit has ballooned to destabilizing levels, those "solutions" are untenable.

Consider the stay-at-home Parent and the working Parent. What both the State and market want is for Mom and Dad to go to work in the market economy and then pay for the services she/he is no longer able to perform: childcare, food preparation, home, yard and vehicle maintenance, tutoring, and so on.

The market wants to provide these services for a fat profit, and the State wants to collect payroll, income and sales taxes on the money now being generated by the working parents.

Is the family better off paying for services that were once provided for free?

As paid work becomes scarce, the question will lose its meaning, for the household income will not be enough to fund market-supplied services for all of life.

In traditional societies that we in America tend to dismiss as "Third World," cash income is scarce and so the vast majority of the goods and services of life are generated at home and by the community.

The home is built with neighbors' help out of local materials, and you reciprocate when your neighbor needs a new roof or house. Food is grown and exchanged for other foodstuffs; surpluses are sold for cash. Childcare is provided by older relatives or neighboring parents, again in a reciprocal arrangement. Schooling is often supposed to be paid by the government, but in the real world parents pay fees to the teacher and for supplies. Healthcare is minimal, with herbal treatments and cheap generic medications providing most of the care.

The local marketplace is self-organizing, and social life revolves around the local church or temple, extended families, fishing or gardening and the market. Cheap mobile phones and Internet connections provide an extended communications network that ties into distant family and friends, news and the wider world.

Cash is needed for schooling, a few food items not grown locally, clothing, mobile phone service and generic medicines. Money is saved up to pay for advanced education and occasional travel via bus or train.

Many of these features were also standard practice in 19th century and early 20th century America.

As discussed in the section on happiness, the secret of a long, prosperous life is well-established: a vibrant social life of friends, family and voluntary associations, a purposeful life (positive reasons to get out of bed in the morning), a diet of whole grains, legumes, fresh fruits and vegetables (lightly processed foods low on the food chain), occasional meat and seafood and sufficient sleep. Olive oil, herbal teas and moderate alcohol consumption seem to play positive roles in the "Mediterranean diet."

None of these requirements require a fortune in cash, and indeed, cash is remarkably irrelevant to social capital such as friendship. (If friendship is based on cash, it isn't friendship.)

Though the State-cartel system is attempting to profit from these "secrets" by distilling various compounds into pills, it is abundantly evident that a healthy lifestyle cannot be replaced by a handful of pills.

A trillion dollars of biochemical research and development will not be able to duplicate the health and well-being of a purposeful life integrated into a caring community and a healthy lifestyle and diet.

The only thing the State-cartel biochemical industry can do for a profit is manage chronic "lifestyle" diseases created by a unhealthy culture. Once the borrowed money runs out, this pipeline of profit will run dry.

We are in a peculiarly new era, one where the positive foundation of community has been lost to the encroachment of the State and market. We need to study the lessons of the past to design a sustainable future. Yet at the same time, the Internet has enabled a radically interconnected, globally empowered community: local services that can be distributed across the globe digitally, ideas can be traded across borders and new technologies and skills made available for the cost of an Internet connection and a relatively modest quantity of electricity.

Let's take a moment and recall the point made earlier about the interstate highway system in 1910 and the Internet in 1980. The idea that a relocalized community-based economy is the foundation of well-being and prosperity runs counter to the ideologies of the two dominant forces in our economy and society, the Central State and the financialized market.

The ways that a Web-powered community can deliver goods and services for a fraction of the cost of the State or financialized cartel "capitalism" are still in the very early stages of development.

The Nearly-Free University

Consider The Nearly-Free University, a development I anticipate will take shape within the next decade. Once the model has been proven, it will rapidly spread, as it is a very advantageous adaptation.

Credentialing is another system that has reached the top of the S-Curve and is slipping into stagnation and decline. What you can accomplish in the real world will rapidly become more valuable than a credential such as a conventional college degree.

The entire education industry on the U.S. is based on an inflexible, increasingly marginal-return "factory model," something I have written about since 2005.

We are "training" millions of people in an assembly-line based on the assumption that academia is a limitless growth industry, when in fact it has reached the zenith of diminishing-return complexity and cost.

The Nearly-Free University may or may not have a physical plant. If it does, it will be a cheap re-use facility such as an abandoned office park or factory. It may not have a physical headquarters at all; "classes" may meet in cafes when the need arises.

The coursework will largely consist of free lectures and tutorials from non-profits like the Kahn Institute or classes already distributed for free online by institutions such as Stanford and M.I.T.

In place of costly professors and overworked, underpaid non-tenure teachers, the instruction will be overseen by part-time mentors from the real world who act as guides, occasionally lecturing but more often encouraging peer-to-peer tutoring and collaborative projects that are not "study groups" but actual work projects that produce something of value in the real world.

The mentor is a working professional who "works" at the Nearly-Free University on a flex-time basis. Their "job" is to suggest a practical foundation of basic courses in the student's chosen field; these courses are taken while the student is engaged in the core curriculum, which are the work projects.

These mentors choose to devote time to Nearly-Free University because they enjoy it; their fee will be modest. Most will work part-time while they pursue their primary career.

Students will move seamlessly from online coursework to projects undertaken in real-world enterprises and communities, learning by doing and from collaboration with others in self-organizing groups.

Mentors would have access (as in the Kahn Institute's classroom software) to a visual display of the student's coursework and work-project progress.

Student would be encouraged to earn money via the work projects undertaken. Instead of owing $120,000 after four years of passive study, students might complete their University experience with earnings in the bank.

Very few people continue on to research or scholarship within academia, corporations or the national laboratories. A relative handful of large research universities would be enough to train those who needed PhDs for scholarship or high-level research. The Nearly Free University model would educate the 95% who do not need PhDs.

Instead of an essentially opaque diploma—what exactly does a diploma communicate about the student's mastery, interests, coursework or accomplishments? —students will be issued a C.V./resume listing all their completed courses and their work projects.

Prospective employers would be able to scan this C.V. and get a real sense of the person's coursework, mastery and work results in the real world.

A decentralized non-profit network of organizations would arise to accredit the coursework shared by the Nearly-Free Universities. There would be no centralized "gatekeeper" that could demand a premium for its accrediting or testing services. Verification of coursework, work history and skillsets would be provided by multiple-sourced, voluntary transparent networks on the Web.

The total cost of the Nearly-Free University might be $3,000 tuition and fees for 3-4 years compared to $60,000+ today. (This does not include room and board, of course.) The credential issued upon "graduation" (an arbitrary concept in an economy that rewards perpetual learning and improved skills) would be secondary to what the student has learned to create, accomplish, fix and innovate in the real world.

There would be no student loans. The low costs of the Nearly-Free University would be paid in cash or hours of labor that the University could "cash" for goods or services it needed to operate in a cash-free labor exchange.

Like many of the concepts discussed in this section, this model is considered "impossible" within the confines of the Status Quo even though it is the only truly sustainable model of universal education.

Three Economic Models: Extractive, Productive and Consumption

As we have seen, the State-cartel model of crony-capitalism is extractive: it extracts revenues and profits without providing any additional value. In this sense much of the U.S. economy is like the "company store," charging an involuntary premium based on monopoly and concentrated power. As noted before, the ultimate monopoly that enforces all private monopolies is the Central State. The extractive model has three components: 1) a Central State which allows extreme concentrations of private wealth which then steer the concentrated power of the State to serve their interests; 2) a centralized State that controls all levels of the economy and State, and 3) a financialized economy dependent on debt, leverage and a highly centralized, opaque financial sector.

Entrepreneurial capitalism based on decentralized, transparent markets for credit, risk, goods and services is productive, as unproductive enterprises soon run through their capital and close their doors.

The non-market community is productive, as it serves needs that have marginal market value, enables full employment and acts as an alternative to corporate-State control.

The State-cartel model depends on ever-increasing consumption that is based on ever-increasing debt. As debt-based consumption increases, that "growth" boosts financial profits and tax revenues.

This model does not need full employment or a productive populace. As long as the top 20% are productive enough to pay 80% of the income taxes, the State can redistribute enough money to lower-income households to stave off social unrest and maintain widespread debt-based consumption, i.e. debt-serfdom. The State-cartel partnership is perfectly happy to pay millions of people to sit at home watching television; its primary goal is to avoid any threat to its concentrated power and wealth.

Unfortunately for the Status Quo, its extractive model of debt-based consumption is beset by fatally diminishing returns: adding debt is no longer adding growth, it is only adding friction, fraud and interest payments. Both debt-based consumption and the centralized Status Quo that depends on it are on the S-curve's downward "last leg."

The sustainable replacement system based on the principles of DATA (Decentralized, Adaptive, Transparent, Accountable) is based on a productive populace, not consumerism. The goal is being productive, not consuming and being paid to sit at home watching TV.

Why is being productive the foundation of a sustainable system? There are two reasons. One is that well-being, health and happiness require a purposeful, socially engaged life, i.e. a life focused on being productive in the community. The second is that an economy with a bankrupt, parasitic State and diminishing surplus must be productive at all levels if it is to be sustainable.

Corporate marketing promised that insatiable consumption (i.e. an insatiable demand for more stuff) would yield not just permanent economic prosperity but individual happiness. As we have seen, it has failed on both counts.

A New Model of the Sustainable "Good Life"

One way to understand a faster, better, cheaper DATA model (Decentralized, Adaptive, Transparent, Accountable) based on everyone being productive is to sketch out an example.

To understand how the DATA model might work in the real world, we must recall why traditional full-time work is in decline: process costs, labor costs and labor time per unit are all in free-fall. Consider software, one of the key drivers of productivity increases. The computer needed to execute complex software code cost $4 million in the 1960s, $4,000 in the early 1990s and today it costs $400. The time required to write, debug and compile most software also declined rapidly as "building blocks" of standardized code remove much of the time and tedium from the process.

Transaction costs are plummeting, as is the amount of labor per unit of production: each auto rolling off the assembly line requires far fewer hours of labor. This is also true of services, where self-service and automated systems are now the norm.

In the pre-mechanization 19th century, roughly half of all American lived and worked on farms. Now agriculture only requires about 2% of the workforce, and even this is still declining. For example, new automated milking machines mean dairy farmers no longer need to get up at 4 a.m.

This automation of human labor is repeating the decline curve experienced in American agriculture: industries no longer need as many workers, and many industries that once employed tens of thousands of people are gone: newspaper classified departments, music and book stores, travel agencies and gas stations. Inefficient industries such as healthcare which spend 40% of every dollar on paperwork are ripe for a similar reduction. Sectors with too much capacity such as retail will also lose jobs as the sector downsizes to fit sustainable demand. Virtually every sector, including the military, manufacturing and finance, is experiencing pressure to lower labor costs and labor time per unit.

The technology-will-save-the-day view is that some new technology such as nanotechnology will create tens of millions of jobs, but there is scant evidence that any material science will create millions of jobs, as high-tech manufacturing is virtually all robotic. Robotics will create jobs, but far fewer than those lost to automation. That is the trend.

There will still be full-time employment in the Armed Forces, energy complex, agriculture, mining, timber, computing, software, manufacturing, transport, research universities and public health and in maintaining our electrical and water infrastructures. But these essential sectors require at best a third of our 200 million-person labor force.

Clearly, the Central State and the market economy are unable to sustain full employment.

The solution is to move beyond the high-cost State/market economy to the low-cost non-market community-based economy where part-time or informal cash work is enough to support a good life because value is being created outside the State and the market.

The sustainable model for 65% of the workforce is what I call hybrid work, a mix of paid and unpaid work that creates value for the worker and the community.

The DATA Model in Action

In the debt-based consumerist model, a three-person household occupied a 3,000 square foot dwelling. In the new model, three households share that space, instantly reducing housing costs by two-thirds. It might be three generations in one home (grandparents, parents and adult offspring) or some variation of that (parent, offspring and a couple of their friends) or three voluntary housemates.

Sharing dwellings and buildings is intrinsically far more efficient and cost-effective than large homes occupied by one or two people. Sharing space also means that maintenance expenses are shared, and some sort of social life and positive reciprocity is built-in.

In the debt-based consumerist model, each household owns a costly vehicle for each adult. In the shared social unit, ten families might share two vehicles, a block might share a pickup truck for occasional use, or everyone has access to a vehicle from one of the many car-sharing companies.

This "access not ownership" reduces vehicle costs by up to 80% per household.

Other transport options include walking, bicycling and a wide range of lightweight, low-cost wheeled vehicles from urban golf-carts to electric mopeds to enclosed tricycles.

Since sickcare (the Status Quo "healthcare") imploded, healthcare consists of limited-coverage catastrophic insurance (no coverage of "lifestyle" diseases that can be alleviated with behavioral changes, for example) and cash-only preventive care. Everyone is responsible for their own health. The cost averages 20% of the old system, an 80% savings.

If the shared dwelling has a mortgage, it is crowd-funded: individual investors reviewed the household's finances and the attributes of the property, and invested directly in a pooled mortgage. The interest and principal is automatically calculated and distributed with open-source software. No bank collects fees or interest.

In the case of a larger building such as an abandoned factory or office complex, the owners do as much of the work as they can themselves and pay for professional guidance. Those owners who have "banked" unpaid hours of labor with the community labor bank can use their "banked" hours to get help from others in the community serving their unpaid hours.

The community labor/goods exchange is a key building block of the community. Those needing labor for any legal, non-exploitive purpose request unpaid labor from the bank. Those with little cash income offer their labor to the bank to "bank" hours of service which they can then trade for other's labor or for goods that have been "banked" at the exchange.

For example, if one of the ten new owners of a derelict building has banked 100 hours in unpaid labor helping others with yard work and tutoring, he can then request 100 hours of equivalently skilled labor from others in the community.

Another new owner might have a surplus of vegetables or fruit from her garden, and she deposits these for free in the exchange, where someone needing the food would offer a certain number of hours of labor in exchange. This owner would then get the labor she needs for the renovation, not necessarily from the person who traded labor for her garden produce but anyone else in the exchange.

The exchange would collect an annual fee of labor, goods or cash from every member, and every member would be required to meet specific ethical guidelines. If any member repeatedly failed to meet their obligations and responsibilities, their membership would be cancelled.

In DATA models (Decentralized, Adaptive, Transparent, Accountable) like the community labor/goods exchange, membership is always a privilege, not a right. The only rights are civil liberties such as the freedom of speech, religion, movement, association and enterprise.

The community labor/goods exchange is a highly flexible, scalable model that lends itself to automated software and transparency. It enables full employment and a largely cash-free non-market economy that flourishes in parallel with the market economy. If someone has cash and wants to hire a person for a wage, they are free to do so. If cash is scarce, the community labor/goods exchange enables every member to trade for other's expertise and labor and local goods.

Severely disabled people may well be unable to contribute, but the majority of people now classified as disabled could contribute in a meaningful fashion. In our example, one of the household members is confined to a wheelchair. In this capacity, he is able to contribute his computer skills to the community and earn occasional cash money. He also provides "eyes on the street" security along with other less mobile members of the community.

Though process costs, labor costs and labor costs per unit of manufacture are all declining globally, another member of the shared household earns cash by working at a local foundry part-time, casting replacement parts at a lower cost than sourcing the parts from overseas. The feedstock is recycled metal.

Twice a month, he volunteers on the local street repaving crew. The city, downsized by bankruptcy and a declining tax base, supplies the materials, equipment and one crew supervisor. The vast majority of the labor is volunteers who "bank" their unpaid hours at the community labor/goods exchange.

Another household member tends the gardens in the property's yards and in community gardens and sells or trades the produce for cash or labor/goods. One of his other jobs is part-time coordinator a farm-to-consumer enterprise that goes out to local farms twice a week and collects produce that is then distributed to members of the group. The produce is then delivered to a pre-selected informal distribution spot such as someone's garage or a church parking lot, where members can pick up their share of the produce. The fees paid by each member of the group pay the farmer an above-wholesale price and compensate the coordinators with a modest cash salary.

Though small-scale agriculture is dismissed in America as "too small to make financial sense," in other countries small home plots, rooftop gardens, etc. supply half or more of the nation's seasonal produce.

Two others in the household are active in the local Nearly-Free University. One is a mentor in 3-D fabrication technologies; the other is studying computer security for mobile devices. The mentor's "class" rents time in the community computerized machine shop/3-D foundry/entrepreneurial incubator to work on their work project, a lightweight integrated frame/body for an all-weather urban "personal vehicle" based on golf-cart technology.

The class project in mobile digital security is to launch a security-enhancement app that would sell for the same cost as a cup of coffee. Any income generated would be shared by pre-arrangement with the University and the class participants.

The student earns money packaging up special-order parts fabricated in the community 3-D foundry for shipment.

One of the residents in the shared household shares a paid job with another person; the 20 hours a week provides enough income to support her entire household because expenses are low. Since she likes cooking, she is part of an informal group that cooks and delivers meals, some for cash and some to invalids as part of the labor/goods exchange.

Her husband is an architect who takes large single-family family homes and transforms them into multi-generational shared dwellings. His other source of income is his specialty sliding-door repair business. His third income-producing project is to coordinate a guild of local craftsmen like himself who each have specialty skills.

Another household member earns cash money by setting up a stall on the pedestrian-only "market" street in the neighborhood. There are three different shifts of vendors per day on the street, morning, noon and evening, and she earns enough in these few hours to fund her household expenses.

One of her other projects is accompanying a friend to monitor local water quality. They sample water at specified locales, take a photo of the readings with her smart phone and upload it to a web server where other volunteers oversee a database of environment data collected by volunteers.

Since the city went bankrupt, it can no longer afford full-time fire department staffers. One of the household is part of the volunteer fire department staff, where he trains with a unit of other volunteers under the guidance of a part-time professional firefighter.

One of his other jobs is crowd-funding projects, assessing the risks, roadblocks and potential yields on various investment opportunities. Some are micro-loans to micro-enterprises, some are artistic projects such as films and others are expansions of successful enterprises. He has earned a good reputation online and receives a small commission of each project that is successfully funded. Neither the State nor Wall Street—or what's left of it—have any control over these micro-investments.

One of his recent successes was coordinating the funding of the community computerized machine shop/3-D foundry/entrepreneurial incubator.

One of the investors works full-time as a researcher on artificial photosynthesis, where the goal is the production of biofuels derived from cheap non-petroleum feedstock. Another investor is employed in the defense industry, designing autonomous submersibles—unmanned submarine drones that will greatly enhance the reach of the U.S. Navy via faster, better, cheaper weapons systems and strategies.

The oldest member of the household joins the wheelchair-bound member in "eyes on the street" neighborhood security and also volunteers in the office of her church.

One of the household's teens has dreams of pop music fame, and his band performs on the weekend pedestrian-bikes-only street fair. Tips from the audience provide a bit of cash, and the band hopes their downloadable song goes viral. He also babysits for cash and helps with lighting/sound in the local theater.

The area also has "intentional communities" in which members share childcare, care of the elderly, cooking, gardening and property security and maintenance on a set schedule. Most shared housing is not this formal, but there is a wide range of shared housing available, including some operated by churches. Many residential buildings rent rooms to travelers or tourists for extra income.

I have presented only a handful of the thousands of enterprises and businesses that are enabled and empowered in a localized yet global DATA model economy and society.

You may have noticed a number of things about this model.

The government, Federal and local, continues collecting taxes, but since the market economy has contracted, so have taxes. The footprint and control of the government is greatly reduced. The Federal government has been downsized to its core duties of defense, research and development, protecting civil liberties and the commons, etc. The local government uses its scarce funds to leverage community volunteer efforts.

The natural selection process has separated the wheat from the chaff in local government; those that enable and encourage the DATA model have attracted the most ambitious and productive residents, while those who protected extractive vested interests (the feudal model) have stagnated into undesirable backwaters.

Wall Street's financialization of the economy and society has also disintegrated; few people or enterprises need big banks or their mortgages and loans any more. Widespread defaults have dismantled the "too big to fail" banks and their machinery of debt financialization. People invest directly in others' enterprises and assets via exchanges that verify and monitor investments and transactions transparently. Debt serfdom is recognized as feudal exploitation, a corrupting construct of the deranging consumerist mentality.

No one is paid to stay at home watching TV. Since the Central State collapsed in insolvency, it is no longer empowered to collect and distribute 25% of the nation's income to its fiefdoms and cartels. Since much of the economy is now cash-free exchange, the cash income of the nation has plummeted even as the well-being and prosperity of its citizens has risen.

No one is retired in the formal sense. Long-lived, healthy people remain productive, and the contributions of the elderly are welcomed and valued. No one is "put out to pasture;" everyone can contribute until the day they are unable to do so.

Most people have hybrid work, a mix of paid, unpaid, self-directed and collaborative projects that yield a steady stream of cash, "banked" labor that can be traded for labor or goods and what economists call social capital. Each person chooses their own mix of productive work. Some will generate cash income, some will not. They are free to adjust or modify their work mix as they see fit; local and Web-based resources to aid them abound.

The cost basis of the DATA model outlined here is very low. Earnings can be saved for future use or invested in a variety of micro-enterprises and projects. The focus of daily life is on productive living, not consumption. The resentful, self-worth-destroying entitlement mentality has evaporated, along with entitlements and the centrally controlled, financialized economy.

The 20% investment that yields 80% of the benefit is the guiding principle in the DATA model. Diminishing returns and malinvestment are no longer institutionalized, they are shunned.

People only change when they have to. As the debt-dependent centralized Status Quo crumbles, what we assumed was permanent will be revealed as temporary. We can resist embracing the DATA model (Decentralized, Adaptive, Transparent, Accountable) and cling to the unsustainable Status Quo until it collapses. In that case, we will have no alternative in place, and the suffering will be both needless and great.

Or we can embrace the necessity of change and understand that the new model for our economy and society is a much more productive and prosperous way of living than the unsustainable Status Quo.

We now know Why Things Are Falling Apart and What We Can Do About It. Let's get busy.

Charles Hugh Smith
Berkeley, California
November, 2012

Made in the USA
Charleston, SC
12 November 2012